DATE DUE

Legal Almanac Series No. 63

WHEN AND HOW TO CHOOSE AN ATTORNEY

by CAMERON K. WEHRINGER

Member of the Bar
of The States of
New York and New Hampshire

This legal Almanac has been revised
by the Oceana Editorial Staff

Irving J. Sloan
General Editor

SECOND EDITION

1979 Oceana Publications, Inc.
Dobbs Ferry, New York

Library of Congress Cataloging in Publication Data

Wehringer, Cameron K. 1924-
    When and how to choose an attorney.

    (Legal almanac series ; no. 63)
    Includes index.
    1. Attorney and client—United States—Popular works.
I. Sloan, Irving J.   II. Title.
KF311.Z9W4   1978   347'.73'5   78-21138
ISBN 0-379-11113-6

Manufactured in the United States of America

TABLE OF CONTENTS

Chapter VI
SUGGESTIONS TO HELP OBTAIN MORE EFFICIENT

Chapter VII

Dedication:

To: My wife, son and daughter

About the Author

Cameron Kingsley Wehringer is an attorney engaged in private practice in New York City and Washington, New Hampshire. He received his B. A. degree from Amherst College and his J. D. from New York Law School. Among other organizations, Mr. Wehringer is a member of the American Bar Association, the Association of the Bar of the City of New York, the New York and New Hampshire Bar Associations, and the National Panel of Arbitrators, American Arbitration Association. He has written legal articles on varied topics including wills, trademarks, and space law. He is the author of "Arbitration: Precepts and Principles" in this series.

Chapter I

THE NEED FOR AN ATTORNEY

The choosing of an attorney to represent an individual is not a choice of clear alternatives. The reason "why" a choice is made may assist or even dictate the choice. An attorney chosen to defend an individual on a charge of murder means a selection vastly different from the choice of an attorney to methodically draw a will.

When the time comes to select an attorney the individual may be under pressure to resolve matters quickly. But generally speaking, no amount of pressure is enough to make a hasty choice.

In the following sections choice of an attorney for different skills is noted. This is akin to selecting a medical doctor. One in general practice is chosen for general physical ailments, and a specialist for that difficulty falling within his specialty.

As with a physician (a medical doctor), if a general practice attorney is chosen, retention of another, a specialist, may later follow depending on the problems and needs as equated with the amount to be expended.

An attorney is needed by most people at least three times in their lives. One general need is for the careful drawing of a will, coupled with intelligent estate planning aid. Another need will be found for an attorney's services is upon the death of a member of the family or close friend, for aid in distribution of the deceased's estate and securing any necessary tax approval, as well as court approval or supervision of the quantity and quality of distribution. A third time generally is upon the "closing of title," the taking of ownership in and to (as attorneys term it) a house and land.

Some people are apartment dwellers and rent. Unless they buy into a cooperative or condominium apartment building,

1

they will eliminate this need, but may profit from landlord-tenant legal advice and analysis.

Probably many people could utilize legal advice for aid in business contracts, leases, and pension rights, as well as insurance coverage review. This last item usually is coupled with estate planning and will drawing or coupled with other property matters. Frequently a good insurance broker will assist in insurance review.

Other people may have more specialized needs. Examples include the securing of protection for a story they write or an invention they create. Others may have traffic court problems affecting their very right to drive. Some few people may face criminal difficulties or find a family-member relying on their help in time of such trouble. Some will have automobile or other "tort" matters. Some persons may have debt collection problems, or the reverse, the resisting of collection by another. A few will need matrimonial legal aid. A limited number may find themselves faced by an admiralty problem. Although all persons are affected by tax problems, not all will find this the paramount need calling for retention of a tax attorney specialist, but on their behalf either their accountant will prove sufficiently helpful or he and his general attorney may utilize such specialist's services on a consulting basis. Trial matters can come to a few, but the retention of this expert may be by the general attorney.

The need is to simplify and not to expand. Gone are the days when a person could claim to be an attorney without schooling or examination. In nearly all cases a thorough preparation has been demanded of attorneys. Yet, this is not to claim, nor to imply, that all attorneys are equally competent or are competent in all fields. The last half of that statement is most important. An attorney exceedingly well able to help on some matters may find ignorance his lot on others. No one can know all.

That all attorneys cannot serve equally well is no reflection on the legal profession. Law is historically and is presently "the learned profession." The attorney's mind is used in other

2

than routine fashion day after day. Scientists have shown that the mind does not age as does the rest of the body; but with use can remain vital and stimulating. Just as some doctors are more capable than others, some dentists more apt in their profession than others, so it is with attorneys.

A competent attorney is not only one that can and does serve well, but especially because of the relationship, the rapport that can be established, will admirably serve the particular client. This points to an individuality of choice, more fully discussed in Part II following.

Why a person needs an attorney can be summed up by noting he seeks a professional man. "Professional" denotes an occupation, if not commercial, mechanical, agricultural, or the like, to which a person devotes himself; it is a calling. The attorney's function is to serve his client. He serves his client as an advocate. His task is to protect his client as against the world, and perhaps even as against himself in certain circumstances.

The professional aid summoned by calling in an attorney should be expected to be high. As a famous American noted, when people are sick, they seek an "uncommon doctor." So it should be that when people need an attorney, they should seek an "uncommon attorney."

The reasons, and the needs, are discussed following.

Will

An attorney should draw an individual's will. The thoughts that go into the will should be the individual's choice. One function of the attorney is to help his client plan his will provisions so that he does what he wants, as he wants, when he wants, but with a view to saving legally the maximum in taxes.

The so-termed will forms that come to public view from time to time are an invitation to disaster. Basically these forms, using impressive type, have a beginning and an end. The form-user is to fill in between the termini the gist of his life's work and final wishes. It is not only what is said, but how it is said that means so much.

3

There is an old example:

Woman, without her man, is a beast.

A comma change brings forth:

Woman, without her, man is a beast.

If attorneys have trouble, and they do as seen from the litigated cases that regularly appear before the courts concerning wills, then the layman cannot expect to give a superior word-performance.

Basically, the attorney will sharpen will wishes. The attorney must ask questions designed to explore a client's wishes in the light of possible contingencies. Some inquiries may be unpleasant. Questions might include a discussion of the client's wishes if the order of deaths is not as logically might be expected. This in turn might include a child's early demise as well as a common disaster causing deaths of all the family. Other inquiries can relate to the possibility of dispute as to items left, the economic abilities of those presumed to survive, and what separate provisions might be of aid, the wisdom of restrictions on immediate giving to those surviving, and other like thought provoking inquiries. The "Testator" (a man who makes a will is called this, and a woman is called a "Testatrix") will be told if there are tax savings if his wishes are varied to some extent. The attorney might note the questionable wisdom of mentioning people in a will whom the Testator does not wish to share in the bounty of his life's work. The use of trusts, created while the person is living or created by his will, may be noted to help do the work desired. Provisions for the children's guardian are among topics to mention to a person who is a family man or woman. For all there is the question of who should serve as an Executor (if a male) or Executrix (if a female) or even a banking institution (the neuter is an Executor also) would serve best. Akin questions may be posed as to the choice of a Trustee. Then, what should be done as to property left to an individual if it is sold before the will comes into force.

All these and related questions can be considered with an attorney.

4

Thus, the choice of an attorney should be one capable and willing to spend time in searching out the individual's wishes and in placing these wishes on paper, carefully and well. The attorney should be one with whom a rapport is established and frank thoughts can be noted. He must not be a person believing a task is for the forgetting after being done.

Choosing such a person cannot be haphazard. It must be done with care. Knowing what the attorney is to do may help in understanding what individual may best serve the particular individual's needs.

Estate of Relative or Friend

When a relative or friend dies, an individual may find thrust upon him the responsibility to see to the estate handling. With a friend this would occur if the individual has been named as the Executor. Also, it might happen if the friend has no will nor relatives and then the individual must see to the estate's administration by the government officials so charged (sometimes called the "Public Administrator"). When a relative dies the responsibility comes by the virtue of being a relative as well as because the post of Executor is that individual's. No matter how, or why, the need for an attorney becomes evident. The attorney is needed to advise as to procedure. This includes seeing the estate through the courts, notifying those required by law, assisting in the tax reports so essential, and aiding in the assembling, administration and distribution of the assets left by the deceased as well as seeing that debts are paid. Some of these duties are charged to the Executor, but in all there may be attorney's aid.

The variety of matters an attorney faces in handling an estate can seem unbelievable. An attorney has been called upon to ward off a paternity claim by forty-year old step-children desireous of being recognized as heirs and so inheriting; an attorney has stepped among ankle-deep papers in the deceased's living quarters to find dividend checks of years past and then tried to piece together the assets of the deceased and of course, collect the monies due and not cashed during the deceased's lifetime; an attorney has negotiated the placement of an abundance of animals in proper new homes; an attorney has helped seek persons whose whereabouts have been unknown for years; and an attorney finds webs of financial entanglements best understood by the deceased who had left no guidelines to follow.

Frequently the deceased will have left his will with the attorney who drew the will. Customarily, this implies a certain trust in that attorney's ability, and an expectation he shall do the legal work generally thought of as "probate." But, that attorney need not be retained for such work. (If a banking institution is named as the Executor, by virtue of certain agreements or understandings between banking and bar associations, the bank will be hard put to bring in another attorney.) An individual is not so bound.

The individual must measure the attorney to the current needs. If the attorney who drew the will is all but retired, as one example, and the estate is both complicated and likely to be of length in probate, another attorney might better aid in this procedure of probate. If there is no will, then there is no attorney who has had knowledge of the deceased's wishes, unless of course the deceased was in the process of drawing a will. No matter; if a will is not executed or not found valid; the law states what shall be done with the deceased's assets and by whom shall the responsibility of seeing to it be exercised. In that case the choice of an attorney is open, and without ties to the past.

The attorney, if an individual is named as Executor, will serve as the attorney and in many instances do the tasks properly of the Executor. (This may explain why sometimes an attorney is named as Executor. However, this neither is a recommendation nor a dismissal of the practice—it is a statement alone.)

The attorney need not be completely familiar with that particular court, nor all its procedure. Many, if not most estates, are handled as office matters, the passage of records through the court being a relatively routine task. The important quality is that the attorney either have the knowledge or the capability of acquiring that needed knowledge without harm to the estate. The attorney should be willing to handle, in fact enjoy the handling of, administrative matters. He needs a knowledge of basic estate law, and an inquiring mind for those points which are beyond his immediate knowledge.

The individual needs an attorney to start from the time the death is known. The attorney must be capable of bringing an order into the gathering together of assets; knowledgeable in knowing whom is to be notified for legal requirements; how contacted; and when.

The tax reports must be prepared. Although an accountant may do the actual accounting, the attorney and the Executor together will see that the reports are readied on time, accurately, and in form correct. The attorney must guide the Executor on the choices that may be in the tax law, perhaps permitting substantial savings to the estate and to the heirs. The attorney must aid the Executor in seeing that the distributions are made in accordance with the will's provisions. Sometimes the attorney must assist in seeing to survivor's immediate needs while the gathering of assets, payment of debts and taxes, and report filing and approval goes on, all with a view to the beginning of a trust operation that is created in the will.

The winding up of the estate means reports to the court, a formal accounting in some instances, receipts and releases from those who have received from the estate, and released by the governments concerned so additional tax claims will not be forthcoming.

If a trust is established under the will, the attorney will aid in seeing that it is correct in law, that the assets needed for the trust are transferred timely and in proper form to the trust, with necessary receipts and releases forthcoming.

If a trust is established under the will, the attorney will aid

All in all, the work is one of time-consuming administration coupled with legal knowledge. Thus, the attorney chosen must be one who can engage in such work; enjoys the work- and will have the time to handle it properly. This means doing what he should do himself and not delegating its performance to an office employee of lesser knowledge.

The attorney will be needed should complaints and outcries of the disappointed arise to any degree. Then advice and guidance are needed to insure that the estate and the remembered heirs are not put in jeopardy.

Should of course the friend or relative die without a will (this is called dying "intestate") then it will be necessary to administer the estate according to the intestate succession law of the particular state in which the deceased lived. This will mean advice is needed as to whom may be appointed as the "Administrator" (the term when a male; "Administratrix" is the term when a female) which is what the Executor is called when there is not a will nor a person appointed to the post under a will. Bonds, and other papers, probably will be needed in such situations. Much of the other work, as with a will, can be the same, except that distribution of the estate will be according to the statutory provisions.

Whether or not a will, or whether or not intestate, if a decedent has property in another state, the attorney will be needed to advise how this is to be handled, particularly if there is a likelihood of a tax dispute by the states concerned. This can occur when the deceased lived in such a way that two or more states could claim he had his principal home (called his "domicile") in each state. In such instances a resolution of the difficulties will be necessary. Also, the attorney will assist in obtaining permission to administer the estate, by the proper persons, in any other states concerned.

The attorney must be able also to assist in determining when a will is subject to challenge. In some states there is community property. In other states there lingers the rights of dower and courtesy (rights by virtue of the married state) under certain circumstances and in certain amounts by each marriage partner in the other's property). Homestead rights (a vestige of the earlier times wherein certain rights in a home are deemed inviolate) may persist. In other states there may be a right for the surviving spouse (the wife -widow- or husband -widower- surviving) to elect to take a statutory amount or percentage of the other's, the deceased's, assets if enough was not given by the will's terms.

These are the problems, or some of them, faced in probate. The Executor and the attorney must work together, even if this is a figurative rather than a literal statement.

Contract

A contract may be oral (verbal) or written. To be written it need not be a long document with "party of the first part" (archaic terminology) or even with formal paragraphing and signature provisions. A written contract (except under certain conditions) can be a letter signed by the recipient as indicating approval, a sales slip, a shipping document, an order book, or other seemingly informal paper; all becoming a contract, written and binding, when signed by the persons to be charged.

In life's dealings all matters can be said to be reviewable by an attorney. But, chances are taken, relying on the faith of the persons with whom dealings are had. Even attorneys, being human, follow this faulty role, and where the amount is not vast will do things they recognize as improper. Examples include the signing of charge slips before they are completed; ordering merchandise based on previous experience as to quality or service and then find the situation has changed; and even signing stock transfer powers for a brokerage house in blank. But, what an attorney will not do, is to fail to review any written paper wherein a substantial sum is involved, or a great inconvenience could be caused. This can be an apt guideline for one not an attorney as well.

A contract, or a series of small contracts that in total are large, should be reviewed when too much is at stake to permit mistakes.

Some contracts cannot be altered. A seller's or buyer's market may exist, and depending in which role the individual finds himself, the best an attorney can do is to advise of the hazards encountered. Then, at least the knowledge of what risks are encountered permits the weighing of these risks against the expected gain. This can lead to an intelligent appraisal of the worth of the matter governed by contract.

Even for the one dictating the terms, or perhaps especially so, an attorney is needed to draw up the terms that can be so troublesome to the other party.

Those contracts that can be changed, or are subject to negotiation from the beginning, are another matter. These need an attorney, not to pass upon what are business decisions, but to insure that what is agreed upon is stated. Further, the attorney should note to his client where there are vague generalities, or even absences of agreement, that could be a potential source of dispute. The attorney can be helpful in advising what the law might be on particular subjects so the parties do not, in all innocence perhaps, contract as to things that would not find support in law.

If, as there can be for certain matters, there are legal requirements as to the signing ("execution") of a contract, then the attorney will see that these aspects are carried out in proper fashion.

The attorney's role in contract matters is that of a counsellor as well as that of an advocate.

Real Estate Closing

Some persons believe that an attorney for a buyer is not needed at a real estate closing if title insurance is obtained. But, that is a vast oversimplification. A title insurance policy says that the issuing insurance company guarantees that the seller can "pass" (this means transfer good title or ownership) to the buyer, but, if something later is found wrong the title insurance company will pay the buyer up to the amount insured, if the defect is not corrected.

However, the title policy contains exceptions. Generally these will concern matters such as the right of a utility company to maintain lines or pipes at or in certain places, as well as excepting from title policy protection certain general laws ("zoning" as an example). The policy also can contain excepttions such as an easement of a neighbor to use a common driveway, or to use what appears to be a simple path. If these examples were not known and understood, the buyer could have planned to block off a driveway, close the path, or whatever, only to find he could not do so. While the noted examples might not prove to be a hardship, these minor matters as well as zoning can affect the plans for property usage.

The attorney for the seller and the buyer are proponents, advocates for the cause of each. The seller's attorney seeks to give away the least possible with the receipt of the most possible. The reverse is the situation of the buyer's attorney.

Clear title, while of utmost importance, is but one part of the matter. It is a question of clear title to what. The sale of a building, such as a house, may bring this into focus. The real property and the building may or may not have certain items therein that pass (transfer) with the house. The seller, if not selling the items, should make certain the buyer has no claim on these; and the buyer, if he excepts the items to pass with the home, must be certain his expectations bear fruit. Thus, each side through the attorneys must define what each side thinks each means. A common understanding is a misunderstanding if it cannot be expressed in writing. What goes with the property may mean different things to each party.

Alterations may be required in a building. Logically then, some provision should be made to be certain the alterations are made. If not made, some remedy might be provided. The seller needs to know exactly what is expected and the buyer must know what can be done if performance does not follow.

Beginning the transaction after a verbal understanding is achieved, a purchase agreement is prepared by the seller for the buyer's signature. This usually provides for the seller to receive a deposit from the buyer, subject perhaps to certain contingencies. The most frequent contingency is the buyer's obtaining a mortgage commitment satisfactory to him. The seller's attorney seeks to firm the sale, so that the deposit monies need not be returned except under specified conditions. The buyer's attorney seeks optimum freedom for the buyer to obtain a mortgage upon the buyer's terms, and make easy the restoration of the buyer's deposit if these terms are not obtained.

11

Assuming nothing occurs to upset the purchase agreement working to a closing, at a stated time the parties meet and papers are signed whereby title to the property is given to the buyer from the seller. At this time the title company checks for any last minute problems that might affect title, the lending institution (if there is one) presents the mortgage papers in exchange for a check, the attorneys check what is termed a closing statement, and a deed is signed by the seller. The closing statement is a financial summary of what is being transferred. It notes not only the basic purchase price but also proportionate costs of insurance policies that may be transferred, fuel oil and other supplies, and anything else that seems pertinent to the particular transaction.

In the buying of a condominium apartment, the comparison in legal work to that of a building (house and lot) is close. In the buying of a cooperative apartment the analogy separates to some extent. The termed "co-op" ownership does not give title to a particular apartment as in the case of a condominium. Buying into a cooperative venture gains the right to occupy, by long-term lease, a particular apartment. (Instead of apartment an office or other usage can be concerned.) This right to occupy is in turn by virtue of certain stock ownership in the co-operative corporation. Problems in co-operative as with condominiums can include what objects within the particular apartment walls pass with the purchase, as well as other problems akin to a real property closing of the type more customarily viewed.

Peculiar to a cooperative apartment in some metropolitan areas can be an ownership separation between land and the building thereon. The co-operative corporation may own the building which is on land leased for a long-period such as ninety-nine years. The attorney, if consulted before any commitment is firmed between buyer and seller, will ascertain the situation. The investment as years pass will be worth less if the land use is leased.

Although the lease of land for a building can prevail in house and lot, or commercial building and other land uses, it would be less usual to find it prevailing in any situation but the more costly ones.

Landlord-Tenant Matter

When rentals are scarce, be they commercial or residential, a renter has little choice but to accept the proffered terms of the landlord. These terms, using an attorney-drawn lease prepared for a realty association with revisions or "riders" as befits the individual property, are designed to give the maximum return to the landlord consistent with law. The need for a landlord to engage an attorney should be clear. Not only must the monetary return be as high as possible, but the landlord seeks protection against tenant's acts or even alleged acts, that can cause damage to the property. The landlord seeks removal of the tenant without a time lapse or difficulty when in the landlord's view this becomes advisable. The landlord seeks protection in the right to renew the lease on the most favorable terms from its view, or even deny a renewal.

The tenant's attorney seeks to gain the most for the least. The rental may have been agreed upon, but what it encompasses, and bringing the understanding down to writing can be a hazardous task. There must be a written agreement as to the condition of the premises when occupancy begins, when occupancy does begin and end, and what the landlord is to be responsible for doing. The opportunity for a lease renewal, or perhaps an option to purchase, may be sought. These illustrate a few of the areas for legal thought.

In some metropolitan areas, where space is at a premium, landlord associations have a "standard" lease form. The word "standard" seems to imply equality and measured choice, being accepted by many tenants with equanimity. "Standard" means nothing. In fact, the situation in New York city became so intolerable that the Association of the Bar of the City of New York, through its committee concerned, drew up a "model" lease designed to be fairer in outlook and approach. The use of such "model" lease cannot be required, but it illustrates the balance that can exist.

In areas of scarce space a tenant may seem to have little choice but to accept the proffered terms. Yet, this need not be so. Landlords and their attorneys may accept certain changes, or clarifications. Even with space at a premium some tenants may be more desirable than others. This intangible factor may persuade the landlord to modify his demands. If nothing else, perhaps the tenant should be apprised of the onerous conditions he may face upon signing the lease. The tenant's attorney should insure that the lease-terms are personal to the tenant, or extend to his heirs, assigns, and successors if that is the situation; he might be concerned that sub-lease provisions are prsent as well. In general he should insure that terms are as agreed.

Another factor requiring attorney attention can include the assumption of the lease by a corporation designed to succeed to an individual business, being the tenant on the lease, and the concommitant release of individual liability.

Where space is not scarce it will likely be the tenant that seeks much and the landlord that prefers to give little. With space not scarce the landlord will seek to induce occupancy by better terms to a prospective tenant. The attorneys' taks is to insure the lease agreement accurately spells out these terms. The tenant's attorney will wish a broad interpretation made possible as to what the landlord is to do, and the landlord's attorney will seek a narrow constriction.

Although what is noted above refers to business decisions, an attorney for either landlord or tenant who is familiar with the problems, or has the imagination to think of what the problems might be, can assist by pointing out various possibilities. Then, the possibilities being noted, the clients can decide how they agree as to the handling. The attorneys' task then becomes one of setting down the understanding.

Sometimes the lease signing will be a formal matter, due to side purchases, or other agreements. In such instances the attorneys will be present to insure that all goes as it should, the parties sign all papers, and the money that is to be exchanged at such time is exchanged. This becomes an administrative legal job.

Debt Collection

Collection of even a just debt can be a trying experience. Resisting an improper claim for collection is no less a problem. Certainly a debt matter that is not clear-cut poses additional problems. For both sides the question usually ends in an attorney's office.

If the parties can compromise their differences; settling the amount owed, or alleged owed, it may be that the attorneys are not needed. But, if the amount is a compromise with bitterness, each side may wish the other to acknowledge that the matter is over, and all relations between the parties have been satisfied. This usually means a "general release" is required. (This is a legal paper saying the signer has no claim against a person or company he names in the paper for any reason. It is sweeping in its legal scope.) Although there are forms for this, and the completion may seem simple, and even be simple, it is of such import that it is essential no mistakes be made. This indicates an attorney should be consulted.

If the parties cannot compromise their differences an attorney arrival for the creditor can make the debtor treat the matter with alacrity. And the debtor, particularly if the claim is deemed unjust in all or in part, must protect himself against legal action. The securing of an attorney by one, means by necessity, an attorney for the other.

Legal papers requiring an answer can be served leading to an ultimate trial of the issues in court. If the creditor is victorious, then the need is for collection. If the debtor prevails, assurance that the creditor is stopped from continuing collection efforts is essential. Settlement along the way can happen, and the creditor should be assured that the settlement is carried out without jeopardy to a return to court if it is not. The debtor needs assurance that upon the settlement being completed the court possibility cannot be raised again.

Whenever court looms, there are intricacies that arise. There are, for example, time limits established by statute (called "statutes of limitations") or reasons in justice why the claim is too late (terms here used are "waiver" and "estoppel"). Always there are procedural points to be observed. This requires legal attention.

Debt collection in the metropolitan areas has spawned attorneys claiming this as a specialty. These attorneys are proficient in appeals of logic and emotion, hopefully leading to a settlement. They have trial ability, a vast knowledge of procedure, and an organizational system permitting a follow-up on an uncollected judgment for the years it remains valid.

The debt collection attorney deals in volume as a general rule. To the extent that the debt is minor in comparison to the time that must be spent in its collection, individual attention cannot be directed. The larger the debt the greater can be the individual approach to the problem. This is not to say that categorization does not do its task. It is to say that to the extent a format must or can be used, it will be used.

Insurance Claim

Many insurance claims involve negligence or tort actions, discussed later. The particular concern here is the presentation of a claim to an insured's own company, and not against a second person (or his insurance company). These might be claims resulting from a fire, water damage, a storm, theft, mysterious disappearance, or damage to an automobile not caused by an accident with another.

In the presentation of an insurance claim the services of an attorney may not be needed. If an attorney's services are needed, sometimes the realization comes after the situation has been fixed with damage to the claimant. The insurance company (or "insurance carrier" as sometimes called) has either attorneys on staff, or attorneys in private practice on call. The company had written the insurance contract with a mind to such legal requirements as may be present, and with a design to maximize the statements from the view of its understanding and its needs.

The presentation of a simple claim, of modest amount, would not be presented by an attorney, or forwarded after his advice. The cost would be too great. But, where a claim is sizeable, consideration to first consulting with an attorney is advisable. The insurance company need not be advised that this is being done; but the fact it is done can be helpful.

Contract language in an insurance policy may not mean what it seems, according to the view of either insurer or insured. For example, some burglary policies, no matter how broad, will have some limits on coverage for certain stated items. One limit may be on "money" stolen from the policy holder, the insured. A claim for the stealing of a coin collection could be claimed to be under the "money" limitation. The claimant would allege "numismatic property" is distinct from "money." Thus, the presentation of a claim should be accurate and note a loss of "numismatic items" and not a loss of "coins." Even so, controversy can remain requiring resort to court action.

The insurance company adjustor who views damage to property should be recognized as in the employ of the insurance company. He is not apt to be generous. He should seek to protect the insurance company and minimize claim payments. An insured's too ready acceptance of his decisions, or a too willing eagerness to give lower than necessary evaluations, would be disruptive of a fair settlement. In some instances the attorney can do no more than emphasize points to note in dealing with the adjustor. In other instances the attorney may assist in the actual claim presentation. The dollar value of loss may dictate the point of effort.

The presentation of a claim itself may have certain formal steps to be taken, and with time limits for each step in the policy. The attorney should review the policy and advise the client-insured to take each step in the required form and in the right time and sequence to prevent refusal of the claim on the grounds it was "waived." Following through on the claim can be a costly experience, but if the adjustment offered is not satisfactory, then action must be taken provided the amount to be gained is not more than the attorney's fees and costs would total.

The action taken first requires that all procedural steps have been attended to, unless the insurance company ignores this requirement.

If there is a dispute the follow-through first may be an attorney's letter; but as insurance companies have staff, or retained counsel, more likely the filing of a summons and complaint to begin legal action will be required. At some point before trial, hopefully, a settlement of value can be made. As some insurance companies are apt to cancel a policy if a loss has been encountered, the attorney will seek to minimize this possibility. The attorney may be able to do nothing, but his view is to protect the insurance holder from prospective dangers as well as to secure redress for past damages and losses.

A trial may be necessary. Then the attorney will be called upon to guide the claimant-client through presentation of the case, perhaps requiring proof of loss, and even proof of the original cost (a hard fact sometimes to prove). The insurance company attorney will seek to minimize loss, and show the claim was excessive.

Traffic Court Problems

A traffic court problem, in the usual situation, in a matter of multi-dollar fine if a guilty plea is entered or if a verdict of guilty is found. In some instances the consequences of a traffic violation can be severe. These include a multi-violation situation or a conviction that could cause revocation of a driver's license. The latter is particularly severe if the driver needs to drive to his work.

In the customary case, where the worst that can happen is the imposition of a small fine, to request an attorney to appear is to make the matter one of principle, with all resulting fees and costs. In the cases where the consequences of a guilty finding would be severe, the matter deserves legal representation. In both cases, an attorney familiar with trial procedures would be most helpful. Choice of the attorney therefore, would be directed to trial oriented attorneys.

Copyrights, Trademarks and Patents

By historical accident, the three fields of copyright, trademark and patent law usually fall together as a specialty (or group of specialities) practised by the same attorney or law firm.

The difference between the three is illustrated by an example. The invention of a better mousetrap may mean a "patent" on the new mechanism can be obtained. To sell the better mousetrap an identification is needed. This permits customers to ask for the particular mousetrap. The identifcation, which can be a word, a symbol, or a combination thereof, is called a "trademark." The advertising and prepared labels for the better mousetrap may include writings, drawings, and even recordings and movies. These are protected by a "copyright," as is this book.

Patent legal work is so involved that there are patent attorneys who specialize in patents concerned with electrical or electronic matters, others with chemical problems, and some with mechanical items. The nature of the invention will determine the type of patent attorney selected. In any patent filing matter the patent attorney will make, or have made, a "search" of the invention to see if it is different from that which has gone before. If it is different, an application to obtain a patent is prepared and filed in the United States Patent Office. After this office, through its Examiners, has reviewed the application, it may object to all or a portion of the application. To this the inventor's attorney must reply. Finally, if all is accepted, the application can be opposed by someone believing the invention, becoming a patent, would damage him. This is called an Opposition. Or, the Examiners can believe another better mousetrap patent application is akin to one filed and ask the inventors to determine who was first, a matter called an Interference.

If all obstacles are passed, a patent is issued. Of course, even then, there is a possibility of difficulty. Someone later might believe a patent should not have been issued and bring an action in court to cancel the patent. Or, if another wishes to use the patent and is willing to pay for its use, arrangement for the payment of royalties requires an attorney. Another's use of a person's patent without permission brings in an attorney to prosecute for patent infringement.

In trademark matters, there is an akin course of events, yet to lawyers there is a different mental attack. This is shown by more and more general law firms having attorneys who will handle trademark, and copyright matters, but not patent matters. An application to register a trademark is filed, this filing being based on actual use of the trademark. If the Trademark Examiner, in the United States Patent Office, believes the mark should not be registered for any reason he will answer, and a reply is required. If the trademark is akin to another trademark being processed, the Examiner may ask that the two (or more) applicants determine who is first by an Interference. If this problem is surmounted, or if it never arises, in due course the Examiner passes on the mark. Then, upon publication as a matter of record, which happens with patents also, anyone can file an Opposition. If the applicant prevails, a trademark registration is issued. Again, later a claim that the registration is invalid can be made and the registration sought to be cancelled. License for use of the trademark, under conditions, and royalty payments, requires an attorney as would the stopping of another from use of the trademark or one similar thereto without permission.

A copyright, on the other hand, is a matter of use with a copyright notice, the filling out of a form, and the filing in Washington. There is not an examination procedure. Only later, if the copyright owner believes another has violated his rights, might an action arise. This would mean an action for copyright infringement requiring an attorney is started.

Each of the three aspects of this specialty (recognized as such by the American Bar Association along with admiralty practice) presents peculiar and distinct problems. An individual or company would need someone competent in the field.

Admiralty

Traditionally admiralty is the second, and the only other, specialty permitted to be so noted to non-attorneys by the American Bar Association. A Proctor in Admiralty is the title carried by attorneys working in this field.

Associated as admiralty has been with large shipping interests, the need for attorneys versed in maritime law seems slight to the layman. With pleasure boating, both on inland and in coastal and open sea waters, the need for admiralty attorneys increases.

The admiralty attorney need not come into the initial negotiations for the chartering of a boat, or the buying of a boat, unless a matter of registry is involved. An attorney competent to handle contract matters can serve probably as well. But, an admiralty attorney is helpful when accidents on waterways occur, or when damage is involved, and he is essential when disputes involve sea usage. Depending on the question, he can be helpful if river usage problems arise. If an accident is involved, the person who is defending should turn to his insurance broker, for hopefully he has been wise enough to secure the services of a broker competent in this area. The broker will turn over the matter to the insurance company attorneys, knowledgeable in this work. If the individual is not insured, or if he seeks the recovery of monies, he should seek an attorney competent in accident work, and adaptable to the understanding of maritime aspects. In a sense, this would be a blending of admiralty and negligence [tort] law work.

Other claims or incidents may be completely handled by a general attorney. To the extent the matter is unique to the water, then an admiralty attorney should be sought for help.

Matrimonial Difficulty

This situation can concern the preparation of an 'amicable' separation agreement, an action for legal separation, a divorce action, or counseling on marriage difficulties leading up to a severance, of any degree, in the marriage relationship.

If defending against a claim, if the insured is fully or properly insured, the insurance company will handle the matter in its entirety. An attorney retained by the insured may not be needed beyond the checking of papers before they are signed, and to be satisfied that the insurance company has full liability, without dollar limitation in relation to the claim advanced. But, if the client is not fully or adequately insured, the insurance company may discharge its portion of liability leaving the defending party with a heavy personal liability. Thus, initially the defending party before permitting complete handling by the insurance company must know if he has full coverage. If the insurance company can retreat behind a limitation, meaning a separate defense, the retaining of a separate attorney may be indicated as wise. Although the ethics of the legal profession state the insurance company attorney, even when the insurance is not complete, must defend the insured as his client, that is, he must consider the insured's interests as paramount over that of the insurance company, logically, this seems to expect too much. The insurance company does pay the attorney his salary, before, during, and after the individual's particular matter is concluded. Separate legal counsel might be advisable.

The claimant needs legal representation in most matters. Perhaps if only a small item, it may be amicably settled, or at least resolved without resort to legal problems. However, as the dollar cost of the damage or injury increases, the resistance to settlement will increase.

There seems substance to the allegation that a "numbers game" is played with insurance claims. To secure even an amount that would be admitted by reasonable people as just and deserved, because of the historical pattern, means an inflated claim is filed. The claim then may lie dormant with the insurance company or its attorneys until action cannot be postponed further. Then it might be settled at the reasonable figure really desired. If the reasonable figure had been presented from the beginning, some allege, then pressure for a compromise from that point would result, leaving only a fraction of that desired.

22

An attorney versed in this field usually has become a specialist to some degree at least. Not only must he know what is possible in the state in which the parties reside, but he must know if the difficulties can be resolved, from the formal legal view, by moving to another state or country to secure legal redress. The attorney must be acquainted with the law as to the obligations of support a man has to a woman, and the children resulting from the union; knowing he may be arguing for a woman in one matter and for a man in another. He must be aware of the tax consequences resulting from the way an agreement is prepared. He must be aware of what happens to an existing will by the action taken, and what rights and obligations as to the children both parties will have.

Logically, the attorney should suggest making some provision for a resolution of disputes which may occur in interpreting the agreement's implementation. Some attorneys suggest arbitration for such quarrels.

Sometimes the attorney in matrimonial matters will be a hard bargainer, perhaps even to the point of disagreeableness. He may be a fighter, beyond reason, for his client, be it the man or the woman. He is an advocate in the full sense of the word, not seeking conciliation or reconciliation. He is retained to represent his client and do the best for him or her.

Tort Action

Tort action refers to those actions usually lumped under the heading of "negligence." It includes automobile accident matters and injuries to persons and damages to property from causes seemingly within another's control. Examples of these items include the alleged invitation to hurt offered to small children by an accessible unguarded swimming pool; the injury caused by a pet defending the family car from trespass where a passerby without thinking tries to pet the dog inside the car; a wild baseball careening off a tree breaking a window and injuring a person; and such other events envisaged in the imagination and finding reality in the doing.

Insurance claims and tort actions are related, as so much that is a negligence action falls under an insurance policy coverage. These matters require attorneys knowledgeable in the practices of tort claims,and congnizant of the practices as to their particular community. The attorney should be called upon before the claim is presented, consulted as to not only the amount of the claim, but as to the method of presentation, and the facts that can be told without jeopardy to the claimant's position.

Trial

Trial has brought forth the excitement displayed in drama, but many trials are routine and painstaking in the extreme. The knowledge of the particular court's procedures as well as general procedural knowledge is essential. Particularly in metropolitan communities, an attorney versed in his field, or fields, may be without competence, or believe he is lacking full ability, to properly handle actual trial matters.

Trial attorneys sometimes are called in, or in larger firms certain partners and associates are responsible for all trial work. They assume the responsibility from the other office attorneys. These trial attorneys are responsible for the preparation and the presentation of the legal papers, the general gathering of evidence and selection of witnesses, making up the preparation for trial, the hearings before a trial is begun, the handling of motions brought by the client, or defending the motions brought against the client, the trial itself,and the details attendant after a trial is concluded. They must know what can be brought into court, and what may not. The logic of a case may not be the same as what evidence or statements are permitted in court. Frustrating as this may seem, both sides share the same limitations, although depending on the matter it may seem one side is more penalized than the other.

The trial attorney, upon completion of the matter, must do whatever is called for to have the decision placed down as an enforceable record. From the viewpoint of the complaining party (the plaintiff) this is to secure the results of the trial.

From the viewpoint of the defending party (the defendant) it is to prevent the issue from coming up again.

The trial attorney and his client may believe that the results obtained should be appealed. This means going to a superior, or a higher, court. Going to such an appellate court is for review of the case with the hope of changing the decision. This appeal may or may not be in the trial attorney's province. Some attorneys specialize in appellate work. There work consists in reviewing what went on below in the trial court (the "record"), considering the legal grounds for contesting the handling of the trial matter and the concomitant result, examining the law in light of the particular matter, preparing and review by the appellate court, arguing in court sometimes as well, and then doing whatever is necessary to formalize the decision reached by this appellate court.

The taking of an appeal requires certain special knowledge and abilities. Although there is not a requirement that an attorney either handle the trial or the appeal, the forms, timing and in general the details are such that those not familiar with the procedure do not attempt it. Some attorneys, or their firms through different persons, can and do handle both trial and appeals. In other instances, retention of appellate-wise attorneys will be sought.

Arbitration

Trial work is not arbitration work although many trial attorneys do handle arbitration matters. Arbitration is a voluntary method of resolving disputes by submitting the dispute before an impartial person who renders a decision ending the dispute. Generally, no appeal is possible.*

Arbitration is characterized by a lack of procedural limitations, the procedure being flexible and designed for full substantive presentation. The arbitrator both reigns and rules, determining the worth of evidence and the value of statements presented. He need exclude none.

*The author's work in this series: *Arbitration: Precepts and Principles.*

25

In arbitration attorneys are not required. The advantages in using an attorney should not be minimized. Some state statutes prohibit an arbitration forum from refusing a party the right to legal representation.

An attorney handling an arbitration matter guides it from beginning to end. He organizes the facts, as an attorney gathers information for trial. He selectes the order and at the proper time conducts his client's case at what is called a hearing. The attorney handling an arbitration need not be one with courtroom knowledge, nor have the flair some associate with trail tactics. Cross examination, a trial art, is more bridled in arbitration. The tempo is more restrained. In fact, it is not unusual for the parties to an arbitration to be friendly, but have a firm difference of opinion. They seek help in resolving this difference, agreeing to rely on the decision (called an "award").

The first need in calling in an attorney is upon receipt of, or when first considering the issuing of, a "demand" for arbitration. Arbitration begins by a "demand" when the parties have a contract stating all disputes arising under the contract shall be settled by arbitration. The first need, when a contract with an arbitration clause is not concerned, to retain an attorney is when the parties recognize the dispute is beyond their own efforts. A "submission" to arbitration may be considered by the parties. In this instance the parties are not required to go to arbitration, but decide that an arbitration would be a better means of resolving their dispute than other alternatives such as an action at law. The parties, with their attorneys, should consider the advantages and disadvantages of arbitration, and delineate the scope of the submission. The scope refers to what issues are to be considered by the arbitrator. This can vary from a limited review to requesting consideration of any and all problems connected with the dispute. Preparing for the arbitration is a matter for care and detail. The question of what evidence and what witnesses exists, as does the order in which the case is to be presented.

At the proper time, the arbitration hearing is held and all the work that has gone before comes to view.

26

When a decision is rendered, called an "award," the attorneys for the parties usually consider that ends the matter and comply with it. In rare cases, rare considering the number of arbitration matters heard and decided upon, a party may believe the matter was not handled properly and have a ground in law on which the award may be upset. In such instances the attorney will seek to set aside the award on one of the limited statutory grounds. In other situations, a party may want the "award" to stand as a court judgment, and will have the award "confirmed" in court. Both of these procedures are usually within the scope of service of the arbitration attorney as they involve motion practice in court as distinct from trial work.

There usually are no appeals in arbitration. There are a few associations that sponsor arbitration that do provide for appeals, but these are rare. Where they are permitted, then that particular association's rules must be followed.

Criminal Defense

If a criminal matter is involved, the attorney chosen should be versed in the criminal law, and familiar with what is done from the time of impending arrest through trial and possible appeals. To the extent the severity of the charge rises, the importance of this statement increases.

A matter involving the dealth penalty as contrasted with a matter calling for a relatively light sentence if guilty, should not call for different talents. As a practical matter it does. The greatest of criminal attorneys cannot spend time on comparatively minor matters. The demand for their services prohibits this. But, careful selection means an attorney who is competent, perhaps a young attorney making his record, as the one chosen to handle the criminal charge.

Tax

Tax matters bring forth the specialist in all his detail. Even though this is an area where a definite expertness is involved, nevertheless as of this writing the field is not recognized by

27

the American Bar Association as a specialty that may be so noted to the lay public. But it is a specialty.

The morass of laws, regulations, cases interpreting, and administrative rulings, have made the matter of taxation a highly involved and time consuming matter.

The tax attorney is used for preventive, and for claimant matters as well as defensive work. The same tax attorney may or may not do all three aspects. Some may utilize trial counsel if this becomes necessary. Others may emphasize an area of taxation. The tax attorney will retain others, or call in others in his law firm, as the need arises.

Preventive tax work refers to the avoiding of tax problems. To avoid a matter, it may mean a contemplated action is not taken. It may mean the contemplated action is undertaken only in a certain way, or with certain limitations. It may mean the action is undertaken without regard for the tax consequences, but being forewarned later tax claimes may be made.

Claimant work includes an individual's claim for taxes allegedly paid improperly. It includes adjustment of what property is subject to tax as well as a monetary recovery.

Defensive work is the resisting of a tax claim. It can be an initial objection to a tax bill, up to an including formal trial of the claim.

The attorney is consulted as to a problem appearing as a possibility when preventive work is concerned; he is consulted as a routine matter as to all things done if possible to best prevent difficulties; and this would include consideration to taxes on all levels of government and in the myriad of forms that have been developed.

The attorney on a claims problems would be asked for his aid upon gaining knowledge that a claim might be made.

On a defensive matter the attorney should be consulted as soon as the situation shows a claim is against the individual. Even a claim for a minor amount might need an attorney, for in the payment the question could arise if this is an admission that leads to larger sums from that government unit or another.

Business

Any individual in business should utilize as a regular matter the services of an attorney and of an accountant. The problems that are faced cannot be listed, for the variety and number can be as the scope and breadth of the business and the activity surrounding it permits.

Although business considerations do involve contracts, all contracts may not involve business matters as commonly viewed. The entering into a business, on a part time basis or a full time basis; by use of the individual's own formula; by the buying of a going business; or by means of franchises; all require consideration from a legal viewpoint.

The form of business is one needing care. The individual may do business under a business name, that is under an assumed name. A partnership may be contemplated with the necessity for careful delineation of the rights and responsibilities of the partners. A corporate form may be selected. The choice of form is one dependent upon general, legal, tax, liability, and personal preferences.

The general legal preferences may encompass the financial or investment advantages, the need for business continuity, or ability to arrange so-termed fringe benefits and consequent individual financial advantages.

The tax consequences can include, and overlap, some general legal preferences including salary and reinvestment possibilities.

The liability aspect can be that limitation the corporate form brings.

Personal preferences can be an acknowledgment of the above, but relying on a decision based on other facts.

Much of the business' legal work may cluster around the formation of the business and in its early days. Not only is the form selected, then formalized, but notification to proper government offices must be made. The proper legends on contracts used in daily business life, the may forms used, and other related items will come under legal scrutiny. The physical place of business may involve purchase agreements or lease forms, as may the equipment of the business.

Continuing business needs include review of the contracts, attention to contracts offered by others for the business to sign, and general legal consideration to the implications of the acts and non-acts of the persons handling the business affairs.

Securities

Even small businesses may seek growth through the issuance of corporate equity (stock) or corporate debt (bonds). To the extent these are contemplated there may be legal formalities to be complied with prior to issuance. On a usually higher dollar scale, the problem of federal law and regulations loom large. The businessman cannot afford to have a seemingly adequate arrangement questioned and undone.

The securities specialist, especialy on the larger financing problems, is capable of coordinating multistate and federal compliances to permit a fund-seeking effort capable of maximum success. Although in smaller financial efforts a general attorney may serve admirably, the larger issue may require the staff, if not the knowledge, of the security-issue specialist.

Chapter II

THE CHOICE OF AN ATTORNEY

Most articles written concerning the choosing of an attorney involve the careful, deliberate civil law choice. The reading person is assumed to be choosing an attorney from many available attorneys practising in firms large and small, practising alone, or even rendering legal service to individuals in addition to customary day-time work on a corporate or other legal staff.

In choosing an attorney, no matter for what reason, the reputation within the community should be considered. This reputation can be of many or singular parts. Civic interests, bar association work and membership, legal aid participation, legal writings, community activities, and general word of mouth are factors that enter into this judgment. An attorney in a larger law firm may be akin to a professional public relations expert in that his working life is devoted to good works. Other partners and associates in a sense share their partner's individual community reputation as their own. Obviously, he fulfills a function in societal structure, but he might be limited in the actual legal work he personally has time to accomplish. However, if the individual inquirer's need is for a firm activity, this should be considered a favorable characterization of the law firm. For the individual attorney, or attorney in a smaller firm, the working day or week must be split. Thus, while some aspects of community reputation can and should be sought, the complete fullness of professional reputation must be equated with the time available for its pursuit. Because of a working life's total time, the younger attorney must offer promise as contrasted to the doings of the older attorney. It takes time to accomplish.

In selecting an attorney, or selecting a firm of attorneys, the choice will be governed by the individuals met or the relationships concerned. The emphasis here is on an individual relationship, be that attorney one of several partners and associates, or relying solely on his own efforts. The individual relationship is one needing fostering and aid. A choice of an attorney for a business of sizeable proportions may have different criteria for selection. Then the choice must be of a firm either capable of handling the volume of work that is contemplated, or a firm willing as well as able to expand by hiring or merger to render satisfactory service to the client.

The individual, in seeking legal assistance, should not be concerned with the size of the law firm. Frequently in a large firm, he will give his problem to the attorney he has chosen, but after he leaves the office his chosen attorney may have the actual work performed by another. Or in the large firm, his chosen attorney will introduce him directly to the attorney who will do the actual work. In what follows, the choice of attorneys assumes that the individual need is paramount, and that any business considerations will be either within such a relationship, or capable of being enlarged to handle the matter adequately.

In each of the seven sections following, the division is arbitrary and notes a different need or a different circumstance causing the need to arise for an attorney.

A Deliberate and Careful Choice for Civil Law Purposes

The caption shows the type of selection. It represents a problem that should have been made before, and is now being made under a sense of need, though not one of urgency. Usually, this will be in connection with the drawing of a will, or complete estate planning. Other examples would include the possible formation of a business, or general assistance on some contract matters that have come to the fore. A hard look at pension rights, from the client-individual view, can bring this to the fore.

The choice is deliberate, for the individual believes and feels that if the attorney is not selected today, tomorrow will do as well. The occasion is civil law, that of office type work and usually preventive law. By doing something, such as drawing a will, something else is prevented, such as the estate passing to unchosen relatives by the laws of intestate sucession.

In this situation the choice is made of many possibilities, or at least of the number of possibilities that are available in that area. The individual should consider all sources possible; speaking to family, friends, accountants, business acquaintances and so on. He might not speak in quest of a particular attorney, but he might inquire how they came to select the attorney they have, and ask what problems arise in dealing with an attorney. The questions can range wide and high, including personality, time delays, fees, and perhaps most perceptively, what is liked and disliked about dealings with attorneys generally and with the particular attorney. Knowledge is sought though there may be no specific questions for the field if one is lacking in familiarity. A sense of understanding is sought, and will be gained even without fully realizing it in talk.

Somewhat Deliberately, But Not So Casually for Civil Law Purposes

This choice is one made with a time-limitation in view. If it is a will and estate planning that promotes the need, the time limitation may be a travel-plan in view. For some reason a change in geographical location, particularly if it is for a period longer than customary, or further away than usual, brings forth a sense of need as to finalizing life's achievement. Another reason may be the pending purchase of a house, or other major consideration usually involving at least the superficial approach to knowing an attorney as he might become advisable.

With this need pending, the choice can be made deliberately, and friends, family, and others can be questioned as to attorneys. The same general gathering of knowledge as to their collective and individual reaction and needs concerning an attorney can and should be sought. However, probably the questions will be more pointed. General questions as to

33

what the attorney does, as contrasted with asking if the attorney does certain work, will be avoided to save time. If a will is needed, questions will concern the attorney's work in this area.

Because there is a time-limitation, efforts to locate an attorney cannot be casual. Some discussions with individuals will be for the specific purpose of locating an attorney now rather than later.

With a Sense of Urgency for Civil Law Defensive Purposes

This situation is illustrated when an individual receives a summons and complaint. The matter may concern a disputed bill, or a claim covered by an insurance policy, or a matter covered by an organization or its attorneys, or other matter with a definite time factor. The matter need not be a formal court action, but it can be a hearing, such as in a tax matter. There the envisaged possibilities looming to the individual outweigh what actually are the more likely probabilities.

In such situations, questions asked of people would go to learning of attorneys who have handled certain situations akin to the problem facing the individual. The inquiry would be as to what can be expected in dealing with the attorney; what would be needed to discuss the matter with the attorney; the costs; and whatever other questions seem relevant to the inquirer.

Although there is urgency, this should not mean the choice is made without care. What it means is that the search is direct and not with leisurely inquiry. There is a time factor. Among the attorneys available a choice must be made within that time. If an attorney who would be preferred will be out of town until after the time needed, then at least someone to handle the matter in the interim must be retained. There can be no procrastination. Thus, the search is deliberate and direct.

With a Panic Stricken View Due to the Possibility of Criminal Prosecution

This overlaps, in some measure, the civil defensive possibilities. Situations where this can occur include a charge of malfeasance, manslaughter while driving an automobile, impending tax evasion charges, or a charge of definite criminal act. The person involved, that is the person who will be defending himself, need not be the inquirer. The inquirer may search for legal help to serve a member of his family or a friend.

At this point friends and family as well as others can be asked for recommendations for an attorney. But, there is little point in vague, general conversation. The questions would lead to what the individuals questioned know, if anything, about criminal law and attorneys knowledgeable in the field. Specific suggestions based on experience would be sought. Probably the questions would be more apt to lead to finding people who have dealt with attorneys knowing criminal law and then asking these people directly whatever seems pertinent in relation to the need.

For Specific Purposes, Such as Inventions or Wills

Although the deliberate and careful view can and usually does include many items, the purpose of this topic is to emphasize the specific need. The attorney selected to draft a will would have a different legal background and knowledge than one chosen for his patent law competence. A trial attorney will have a different legal approach and knowledge than would a tax law expert. The purpose in such instances directs the choice of an attorney. A trial matter would be a purpose leading to the seeking of a person with trial ability foremost. A labor matter would require the seeking out of a person capable of coping with such problems.

The choice then is a focus upon specific abilities. This narrows down the choice from all attorneys to those with competence in a particular area or areas.

Sometimes, if the need is specific enough, or if the area is served only by general attorneys without specific fields of knowledge, the inquiry will take the individual geographically far afield.

In a Small Town (Rural or Suburban) Among
A Limited Number

Generally, the numerical possibility of choice is limited in a small town. The reason for need cannot be as selective as where there are numbers available from which to choose. An attorney would be considered as to his relative ability in relation to others who might serve also in the most general of ways.

Even in a small town there can be variables. The attorney actively serving would be most helpful in all likelihood in matters involving a day-to-day relationship with various town people. By choice his work is of the broadest offering probably, emphasizing that which most people might need in a routine fashion. Certainly for a court appearance in the area he logically would be known best and capable of achieveing the needed result.

On the other hand, neighboring towns, or nearby cities can be considered for work of either a more specialized nature or where an impersonal need is sought. Even though the attorney does keep client confidences to himself, to some persons it is easier even not to meet that person so knowledgeable of their innermost confidences on any regular basis. Therefore, an attorney not available regularly for casual meeting will fulfill an emotional need.

Besides the neighboring towns, and nearby cities, there may be other attorneys whose office may be elsewhere, they choosing the area for a second-home, or there may be those who are semi-retired but with unique and specialized knowledge and abilities. Such attorneys might be willing to serve. If they are not admitted to practice in the particular state, then their services must be on a consulting basis with a local attorney. Certainly if the problem presented seems to warrant the consultation of this other attorney, then the attorney regularly serving the area should not object. His concern should be and is to see that his client is served best.

The emphasis in rural or suburban areas usually is on relative or general competence as contrasted to a highly developed specialty of law practice. In both rural and urban locales the intangibles of attorney-client rapport, community reputation, and impersonal dealings are of the highest importance.

In a Large City, With an Abundance of Impersonal Choices

In theory at least, the large city should offer the widest possible choice. There should be attorneys practising broadly and serving as general attorneys and others with a narrowly constricted area of legal expertness.

The urban area should mean that all avenues of inquiry as to an attorney, all aspects of choice, can be had. In the last analysis, an individual lives his life in a group. Thus, the attorneys known to those comprising the group will be but a few among a larger number of many attorneys admitted to practice. The individual's circle of friends, acquaintances, and those questioned, may find attorneys' names being repeated, thereby giving him an actual choice of only a few.

The difference from urban to rural is that if the individual were so inclined, upon finding attorneys' names being repeated by members of one group, the inquirer could find another, even diverse group of people. In urban life, many are associated with different groups for different needs. With the exception of the individual concerned, frequently these groups have no connection, one with the other. However, rarely will an individual go to a strange group to make inquiries. Thus, a choice of attorneys will be from those recommended from as many groups as the individual is a part. It will be broader, larger, in number and diversity perhaps than offered the rural inquirer, but it is not as large in total as one might think.

Chapter III

WHAT TO EXPECT OF AN ATTORNEY

An individual should expect the most from an attorney. An attorney should expect to give no less.

An attorney is a professional person whose function, if perfectly performed, is to serve as well as his abilities, his strength, and the individual client permits. His first concern is to the client.

Examples for discussion follow.

Attention to Problem

An attorney should be expected to give his best attention to a problem presented to him. An attorney should not be expected, nor asked, to give a superficial response and then held to the answer as though it had been thoroughly and painstakingly prepared.

Attention to a problem means in theory giving more time than the problem seemingly warrants. Even a simple question requiring a simple answer can be wrought with complications. An attorney should try to note what possibilities there are to the client's problem. Frequently a client will believe his matter is the essence of simplicity, but it actually is not. An attorney should think of the various factors that do or could affect his client's position, and what can should be the alternatives of action considered.

From the attorney's point of view, attention to a problem means not dismissing the problem after law-office hours. Some of the best solutions to problems have come at odd times (even in the midst of showering) as they arise from subconscious activity on the client's problem. Attention to a problem means consideration not just to the extent the client requests, but to the extent the problem demands. Attention to a problem means a willingness to bring forth suggestions in connection therewith that may be at variance with views earlier expressed to the client and thought final. Attention to a problem means a willingness to reconsider after a matter has been terminated, so that better action and service can be given to the same or similar problems in the future.

Law is a process, a continuing process of learning. To the extent learning is sought and obtained, service is given.

Amount Concerned

An attorney's proper attention to a client's problem requires time in any situation that is not completely routine. And even a seemingly routine matter may have its complexities. Time is a charge. It is unfortunate perhaps, but in minor matters it may not pay to engage an attorney. Lest the individual believe this imparts a cost element out of proportion to justice, analogies in all phases of life can be seen where the cost of repair may not equal the cost of replacement. In essence, the cost of attorney-work rectifying problems may be more than the cost to write off the matter and begin anew.

One reason for the time problem is the inexactness of law. Law is a constantly evolving thing. Evolution is brought about by legislatures, by administrative bodies, by judges, by hearing officers, and by executive orders. For example, the doctrine of freedom of speech is set down in the Constitution. Yet this does not mean, according to a famous jurist, that a person may cry "fire" in a crowded theatre. So it is with laws, regulations, and rulings on more complicated subjects. There are interpretations, restrictions and evaluations. An attorney must know and sense when differences arise and need review. Review takes time, and time is a cost factor.

Report of Action Taken

An attorney should report on the status of a matter from time to time. A client should not be required to request a report on changes made, delays encountered, and generally keep his client informed. A client has the right to insist that information be forthcoming.

In all instances where a dispute is concerned, the possibility of settlement may be involved. An attorney cannot make a settlement without the approval of his client. The attorney should report back to his client and give his opinion of the wisdom of accepting a settlement offer, or of rejecting it either with a view of negotiating further, or even terminating negotiations. In some instances the opinion the attorney will give is not so much a legal view as an evaluation of the perspicacity and tenaciousness of the opposing party. It is not unlikely that the client may be best able to make this evaluation. Here cooperation is needed between the parties; a cooperation based on the understanding of human beings as human beings. The matter is not one only of legal interpretation. The attorney in settlement negotiations may note to the opposing attorney that he will recommend acceptance of a settlement offer. This is proper. But, it does not mean the client must accept the recommendation. It does mean the attorney's judgment is that it is the best settlement at that particular stage of events. The attorney may realize more can be obtained, but that the cost of obtaining a higher amount would wipe out the gain. This would lead to a recommendation to his client to accept the figure.

The attorney can report to his client in ways best suited to their relationship. In some instances an attorney may prefer the telephone; in others a letter; and in some cases forward a copy of whatever communique has been received. The choice should be one made best to put down for ready reference, both to the attorney and his client, the status of the matter and to permit speedy action when necessary.

Best Interests of the Client

The attorney should not be expected to sit in judgment on a client's problems. His position should be that his client has retained an advocate, a champion, and he is to advocate, to champion, his client's cause. This does not mean the attorney should agree with his client. In fact, between attorney and client there may be deep discussion as to a proposed course of action. But, as to others, there should be unity.

An attorney who finds he cannot continue to represent his client, for any reason, cannot resign without first insuring that his client has an opportunity to secure adquate substitute counsel. The client, on the other hand, needs no reason to dismiss his attorney. The client in dismissing his attorney may find his attorney does not cease work. The client must be protected. This is foremost.

The attorney's obligation is to continue to exert his best professional efforts on behalf of his client until other counsel has been obtained, has familiarized himself with the matter and has been substituted as counsel with the client's approval, and where applicable, with the court's approval. An attorney may not merely leave a matter abruptly.

Confidence of the Client

There are three professions where confidences between the individual and the professional man must be inviolate. They are the professions of law, medicine and religion. Only the client is permitted to release the confidential situation.

Confidences of an attorney-client relationship begin before this relationship is established. An individual should feel free to reveal his problem to an attorney with a request that he undertake the matter, and upon that attorney's declining, not be concerned that the attorney will reveal what has been said.

The attorney need not accept a client, and a reason need not be given. But, the information given leading up to that decision is as sacred as the information given when the client has been accepted.

42

Fee

The attorney has a right to his fee. The client has a right to an understanding of the fee. To the extent that it is possible to discuss this beforehand, this might be done. In instances when it is not possible, because it is a time and advice situation, then the client has a right to inquire if the client believes it necessary, for information as to the time spent, and even particulars of how that time was spent.

The fee should be paid as promptly as possible. If the matter is such that the fee cannot be paid at once, frank recognition of this should be given to the attorney and mutually satisfactory arrangements achieved. Generally speaking, if a client pays his statement within ten days, this would be excellent practice.

Chapter IV

WHAT DOES AN ATTORNEY COST

As Lincoln noted, "A lawyer's time and advice is his stock in trade."

It is not possible to duplicate time, although it is possible to duplicate advice. Even if advice is obtained from several attorneys, and it varies not an iota, as each attorney spent time in the rendering, each attorney should expect compensation.

Time is a relative factor. One attorney may spend much time on a problem unique to him, and another in a much shorter period of time present the same answer. Yet, the fee statements need not be too different. In the one case the time factor is at its lowest increment. In the second situation, the time factor charged is higher due to the acquired experience. There is a relationship between the time and the effective use of time. Although some attorneys may have a flat hourly rate, somewhat in accord with their years of practice, the field of knowledge in which they practice, and the custom of their community, other attorneys will vary the individual time charge depending upon the novelty of the problem, its difficulty, the degree to which it precludes consideration to other matters, the value to the client, as well perhaps as the attorney's inward feeling of efficiency toward the client's work.

An analysis of some of these facts shows some of the reasoning behind the consideration.

The years of practice of an attorney should bear some relationship to ability. Practice in a field should aid proficiency. This should bear some worth to a client, and is charged accordingly.

The field of knowledge carries its value as expressed in a time charge. In a field where there are few knowledgeable persons, the seeking of answers to questions in that field usually means a higher cost than in a field where many are thought competent to reply.

The custom of the community is a factor that cannot be dismissed. The difference is not so simple as the difference in living costs between rural and city, or between different areas within this country. The difference within a seemingly homogeneous area, or within a city, can present pronounced cost variations. This is true in many service aspects and can be no different in legal work.

The novelty of the problem carries its price. If the problem presented is one without precedent, and where the attorney must "make law" (as the expression is) then this will require a handling other than routine. The uniqueness, while being appreciated by many attorneys for the challenge value, is borne by the client in its solution.

The difficulty of a problem is related to cost and to time. If a problem has its own problems, not necessarily novel ones but hard thought matters, then it cannot be handled as may be a routine or easy item.

The degree to which the client's matter precludes consideration to other clients' matters should be more or less self-evident as a cost factor. If an attorney is required to be absent from his office, so that he cannot attend to another client's problem, his time must be charged to the client requiring his office-absence. It cannot be of concern even if the attorney may effectively work for the billed client for only a short period of time during the absence from his office. The attorney may spend time traveling, waiting to see other parties, idle time waiting at a hearing, or practice patience in other ways, all taking time. The total absence-time must be tallied, and billed.

The value to the client can be noted along with the principle worth of the matter to the client. A client pursuing a small dollar item for the sake of principle cannot expect the attorney's fee to be equated to the smallness of possible dollar recovery. For example, a dispute involving even a hundred dollars could easily take up a hundred dollars in billable attorney's time. If the attorney were to charge what the time and effort were worth, then his fee would be more than the dollar recovery. The alternative is to expect the attorney to work for less than his time is worth. In such matters the client would be well advised to suffer the loss, real or imagined as the case may be.

On the other hand, a client pursuing a small dollar item, and following the attorney's advice even when it seems to mean a non-profitable settlement, should not expect a fee unrelated to the dollars involved. Also, a client pursuing an item that may be small in itself, but which finds a duplication in a series of identical contracts and involves perhaps many dollars in total, should expect that the value of an able attack on the problem will bear a fee charge related not to the one contract, and although not necessarily to the probable series total, the fee will bear a reasonable relationship to the time cost expended.

Forwarding Fee

An attorney forwarding, sending on, a client's problem to another attorney for any reason sometimes receives what is termed a "forwarding fee." Although this is not to say it is approved, it is a fact. By intra-office law firm accounting, the same system may prevail; that is the partner the client sees may pass on the work to another partner for solution. Each partner may receive an agreed upon percentage of the total fee. The "forwarding fee," while identical or similar to some law firm arrangements, nevertheless is differently viewed when between or among attorneys who maintain separate offices.

When an attorney forwards a matter to another attorney while still keeping supervision in any degree, he may be serving the client and should receive compensation for this.

The forwarding fee is expressed usually in terms of a percentage from the receiving attorney to the sending attorney. It is logical to assume this means a client-bill markup is arranged to pay this fee; but this is not necessarily the case (no more than it is intra-office forwarding). The percentage is

47

accepted by the receiving attorney as a cost of practice just as are rent, supplies, and employees.

Generally, the forwarding fee comes into view when a matter is referred to a specialist, or to an attorney in another geographical area other than the one in which the sending (forwarding) attorney practices law.

Among some law firms and attorneys, a scrupulous practice of not paying forwarding fees to outside-the-firm personnel is followed. There can be, but not necessarily is, a benefit to the forwarding attorney. Nothing so crass as money or gifts are involved. If the other firm is either in another specialty or located in another geographical area, the habit, so to speak, can arise of sending all business appropriate to such other firm to that firm. Reciprocity is shared.

Flat Rate

In any field of endeavor, customs and practices arise. Some of these customs and practices relate to costs. In law, at least as to certain geographical areas, there are customs as to fees. Some are on a "flat rate." The flat rate, or flat fee, refers to a basic dollar charge for the performance of certain legal work. To this fee may or may not be added disbursements, which would be the only flexible variant.

The usual use of "flat rate" charges seems to be where there is a regularity or form type of situation. This would be where an attorney files a regular form, even though modified for individual situations; or where an attorney does a certain type of work that has a repetitive aspect to its performance. By way of example may be cited the preparation of a federal trademark application. Many attorneys versed in this work quote a "flat fee," to which is added the government filing fee and other out-of-pocket costs.

Percentage

A percentage fee is fixed in certain matters, by custom and by ease for both attorneys and clients. The percentage is fixed as a full and adequate fee, for matters in which an ending is not known. To it, of course, are added disbursements in many instances.

An example is a real estate closing. The attorney's fee is fixed as a percentage of the price of the property. In estate matters the attorney's fee usually is a percentage of the gross estate. The reasons can be rationalized or dismissed as historical with present day carry-overs. The point is that they exist. The percentage may vary from one locale to another. In some states the attorney is expected to certify that good title (ownership) is transferred and title insurance companies do not enter into the picture. In those locales the percentate is higher than where the attorney does not attend to title certification, but relies on a title insurance company and the policies it issues.

To those who would criticize the percentage system as being unfair, and perhaps sometimes they are correct and sometimes they are not, can be noted the rationale of value to the client, coupled with the time spent. At least, unlike a sales tax that remains constant with increasing purchases, or unlike an income, estate, or gift tax that increases in percentage terms with the increasing dollars, the percentage of an attorney usually at worst stays constant, and at best diminishes with the increasing dollars involved.

In estate matters there is justification even today, no matter what the historical antecedents, in that an attorney's fee based on time would fail if either court approval or tax reports were involved. And, except for minor dollar estates, these are concerned even when the assets are primarily what are termed "non-testamentary" assets, such as life insurance policies. With the filing of a tax or court report, the attorney's fee must be set down. If, after the undetermined time spent in achieving approval of the report, the attorney were to amend his fee, then an amendment of the report would follow. The amendment of fee would require an amendment of the report, requiring an amendment of fee and of report, and so on. This indeed would be ridiculous.

As to real estate closings, the present day rationale is not as clear. There are no tax or court reports in the customary situation. But, the custom lingers, and can be compared on very favorable terms with the real estate brokerage commission; the latter usually being several times as large in any one transaction, and involving (from some attorneys' views) less responsible.

There are other miscellaneous matters where local custom may dictate a percentage fee statement. In adoption matters, where the private adoption agency is concerned, its fee will bear a direct relation to the income of the adoptive parents. The attorney, in turn, may request a percentage of whatever fee the adoption agency required. This avoids the placing of time-dollar value on a new family member.

Time and Advice

The time and advice charge, with the interrelationships noted above, is the more customary method. Then the time charge, which as earlier noted varies not only as to the attorney charging, but perhaps even according to the particular matter and the efficiency at a particular time of the attorney himself, is used for computation. Many attorneys set forth a minimum fee per day on a time charge. Thus, a letter or telephone call might not equal a unit of time charge (be this unit one-fifth of an hour, that is twelve minutes, or one-quarter of an hour, and that is fifteen minutes) but for that day the minimum would be as though the minimum time had been spent. Little imagination is needed to surmise that a frequency of minimums can be more costly to a client than a more selective use of the attorney's time.

The advice factor can vary with the amount concerned. A leader of a metropolitan bar regaled attorneys with the story of a telephone call that cost the client several thousand dollars. The attorney when questioned by his client, noted that a large profit in a multi-million dollar transaction depended on the attorney's reply. The attorney opined that the few minutes spent, considering the risk, meant the cost of his advice was realatively modest. Apparently his client agreed, for the attorney claimed his client continued the relationship with him.

Advice is a nebulous concept that needs careful consideration. An attorney called in, knowingly or unknowingly, to review the ultimate conclusions of another attorney, and who makes no changes, has a valid claim to as substantial a fee as if he made changes. The confirmation, being an honest evaluation, is worth money. The fact confirmation was needed, if one thinks about it, even could be worth more than the original fee paid another for the original answer. If the original answer were thought satisfactory, confirmation would not have been needed; so the reassurance being given by another most assuredly in the focus of scrutiny, should be increasingly valuable.

Principle of the Matter

This has been noted in context of other sections. When principle is involved, the fee relationship to the dollar sign of the matter cannot bear consideration. Someone who is deeply concerned over an unjust overcharge of a few dollars, and is willing to consider definite legal action, must be prepared to pay on a time and advice basis unrelated to the original amount concerned. The matter can involve a minor dollar overcharge from a business, or a traffic ticket (unrelated to a possible state's point-system negating the right or privilege to operate an automobile) or another minor dollar matter. If contested, using an advocate's time (an in this instance most clearly is the role of an attorney seen as an "advocate") then the cost must be borne.

The person retaining the attorney must understand clearly the dollar question originating the suit can be and probably will be eclipsed many times when principle is the reason for contesting. The client has the right to and should inquire ahead about probable legal expenses, but if he engages the attorney to pursue the matter, he should be exptected to pay the statement rendered without comparison to the dollar result.

Will

By custom, if nothing else, the drafting of a will usually is a cost to the attorney and not to the client. Some attorneys charge a minimum fee, or something closely related to it. Some attorneys, recognizing the out-of-pocket expenses that will be incurred, insist that any and all disbursements, including proportionate stenographic charges, be paid by the client. In no other situation is there the regularity of a bargain as in the drafting of a will.

The lower-than-actual-cost in drafting a will assumes as a general rule that there are no special problems arising; that a trust is not created by the will; and that a minimum of the attorney's time is requested.

Obviously, if even the simplest will is drafted only after a multiplicity of telephone calls and other demands upon an attorney's time, this low fee custom cannot be and should not be followed. But, if the client is direct and works with his attorney, there is scant reason to expect more than a customary low bill for a simple will assuming the individual attorney follows this as custom.

A will that is not simple, encompassing within its framework the creation of a trust, or involving a marital deduction, or dealing with several bequests and charitable considerations, usually involves a greater charge. This greater fee may be slightly more or in direct relationship to the time and advice factor. The particular circumstances will determine what is to be.

Attorneys concerned not only with drafting the will, no matter how complex, but also with the total evaluation of the estate and a recommendation of the best way or better ways to reduce potential taxation, can aid the client in the out-of-pocket costs the client must endure. The will can be billed at a relatively modest fee; but an additional statement can be tendered for "estate planning" (which is assuredly the most vital aspect). The second, and larger statement, is a tax deductible item. Thus, whatever it may be must be related to the client's income tax bracket. At the end of the client's tax year, the income tax percentage of the fee is in effect 'paid' by the government in the form of a tax deduction. In such situations attorneys should be expected to charge more nearly if not the worth of the time and advice given; although historical patterns die hard and some fail to do so. An attorney who does not so charge can be reminded of his lapse without great financial hurt in the real sense to the client. The client should gain thereby the attorney's appreciation for this recognition of legal services rendered.

Estates

Estates are matters where a percentage of the total gross amount is usually the fee. This percentage frequently is based on the amount reported for taxes, if applicable, before exemptions and deductions.

Misunderstandings can occur at this point. For example, where an estate is made up of testamentary amounts (meaning items passing by will) and non-testamentary things (items passing by contract including insurance, but possibly taxable and surely reportable), questions can arise. The governments know a named beneficiary of a non-testamentary item, such as an insurance policy, can be a means of tax avoidance (correct enough as contrasted to the evil of tax evasion). Thus, a reliance on non-testamentary matters named to other than the deceased's spouse or other principal beneficiary, when the spouse is named Executor, cannot be a means of avoiding attorney's fees. For example, if a person dies leaving an estate where one-tenth passes to one person, and nine-tenths to another, the total estate is the basis for the attorney's fees. Otherwise, it could become bargain basement shopping for an attorney. That is, the one-tenth recipient would seek the attorney (relying on the fee being based on one-tenth) rather than the nine-tenths beneficiary retaining the attorney.

The attorney's fee is payable at least by the time the tax return is filed, for in most tax returns the line setting forth the attorney's fee refers to fees actually paid. In larger estates, and the term "larger" is relative, the fee may be paid in installments, some being paid after a certain amount of progress has been made; another portion later, and so on. In all instances, the attorney's disbursements are an additional obligation.

Where the will does not permit the Executor latitude in payment of the fees, state statutes may permit the attorney to request court permission for partial payment. Even when latitude is not expressly set forth in the will, when the recipients and interested parties to the deceased's estate are not at variance, the Executor can permit partial payment as benefits the circumstances.

The precentage amount of the attorney's fee not only varies according to the amount of the state, but can vary according to the area even within the state. It is not accurate to say that a rural attorney's percentage fee will be less than a city attorney's percentage fee. It is accurate to note there can be differences depending on the locale. An area of abundance and wealthy persons reasonably might expect that attorneys, as all others, would receive higher fees than attorneys performing identical work for persons dying resident of economically depressed areas.

Further, the attorney's fee can vary according to the Executor appointed. If a professional executor is appointed, such as a bank, the attorney will perform strictly legal functions. When an individual is named, such as a deceased's spouse or lay relative, as a practical matter the attorney will perform both functions. In the latter instance the attorney's fee can be expected to be somewhat higher as the attorney must consider the greater work and responsibility he will handle.

If an attorney is appointed as Executor, in which case it is logical to expect he will handle the legal work, the total percentage of the Executor's and attorney's fees can be expected to be less than the total of an Executor's fee paid to one individual (or banking institution) and one attorney's fee paid to an attorney.

When an attorney draws a will he may expect he will handle the legal work for the estate that later arises. That expectation is increased if a banking institution is named as the Executor. The reason is there are in some places an agreement, written or understood, between the banking community and the bar associations. The agreement provides the bank will retain the attorney who drew the will to handle the estate legal work, barring a compelling reason to the contrary. Thus, an attorney can achieve a relative certainty of future legal work by having banks named as executors in clients' wills. To expect the same certainty of understanding with individuals would not only be impossible, but if sought to be achieved might be a violation of an attorney's professional ethics.

Contract

In discussing the attorney's fee and the contract, much depends on what the attorney is to do. If he is to aid in negotiations, finalize the thoughts from both a business and legal view, and then draft the contract himself, the time and advice charge should be expected. If the attorney is asked to review a contract already created, the attorney may charge by time and advice or even note a flat rate.

The elements going into the time and advice billing must relate to factors noted before. As said before if the contract is relatively minor in dollar amount, the fee should be expected to be minor. But, if this same minor dollar contract is one of a series of similar contracts, which total many dollars, the fee cannot be expected to be small. Also, if the contract is a pilot, or first contract, in a projected series of contracts, the same comment applies. Even a minor dollar contract that is contested on grounds of principle means the face value bears no relation to the attorney's fee.

A contract of major dollar important will bear a higher fee. It is not that the higher dollar automatically means a higher fee, it is that with the potentialities of problems the attorney knows he can spend enough time to fully satisfy himself and his client.

Real Estate Closing

The charge in real estate closings is usually on a percentage basis. The percentage usually is a mere fraction of the broker-

55

age-fee percentage. Both buyer and seller have their own attorneys, each to watch after the parties' respective interests. Even so, the total legal fee is much less than the customary brokerage fee.

For the fee, barring law actions or other complicating matters, the attorney represents his party up to an including the charge of title. "Title" means the fact of ownership. A person has title, or ownership, in real property. This representation can involve little or much work. It can be difficult legally or routine in the extreme. When an attorney undertakes representation of a client in a real estate closing, as in an estate matter, he usually cannot anticipate if difficulties will be present requiring a heavy or light time expenditure.

A logical reason for this basis of legal fee charging is to permit the parties to know what the costs will be. The brokerage fee, the title insurance policy, and the attorney's fee are all percentages. The necessary insurance policies against hazards are equated to the value of the property as are the taxes levied. Thus, the pattern is uniform.

In some states, or some areas, title insurance policies are not usually used. In these locales the attorney will certify the title. This means he will search, or have searched, the ownership history, check on any claims against the property, and then give an opinion as to the title. In such situations the attorney's fee must be higher than where the title is backed by a title insurance policy.

Landlord-Tenant Matter

This is a field of bitterness according to many; and one where many attorneys insist that the fee, or a large proportion of the fee, be paid prior to work commencing. The fee, taking into account the worth of the matter, may be expressed in terms of a "flat fee" or a range for certain legal activities as discussed between attorney and client. The fee may be based on a strict hourly charge, with a retainer amount requested prior to work beginning.

A percentage amount is relatively rare. The attorney for the landlord, if he represents regularly the landlord in landlord-tenant matters, may not require either a retainer or outline the range of the fee. If the attorney is on a retainer to attend without limitation to the landlord's needs, the attorney will handle the matter to the extent necessary dictates without additional cost to the landlord.

Usually a hearing or a trial action may be contemplated in landlord-tenant matters. This is considered in the estimate of a fee given by the attorney for the tenant, or for landlord if not handling the matters on a regular basis. However matters of appeals from hearings or trials may not be contemplated in the estimates.

Debt Collection

Debt collection in the larger metropolitan areas is a specialty. Attorneys versed in the field are trial men knowledgeable in every procedural nuance and methods of obtaining assets where seemingly nothing was available. They are calculating in benefits to a client.

The fees generally are a percentage. The percentage may be from one-quarter to one-half of the recovered sum, or staggered depending upon the amount received. In addition a retainer is requested, against which the attorney's fee upon recovery usually is credited.

Unscrupulous debtors without an adequate defense, knowing of this arrangement, will offer a needful creditor an amount to settle an amount that is just under the attorney's portion. The argument is that the creditor will prefer some money immediately, and receive at least something more than the net sum would be after legal action.

The debtor's attorney will handle his defense on a time basis, flat fee, or without a given range. Because of the amounts that can be in issue, either side's attorney frequently can and does, advise settlement at an early stage. If they find that success by the creditor is likely it makes sense for the debtor to pay an amount that is less than the total amount even when added to the amount that will be out of his (the debtor's) pocket for his attorney's fees. And, it makes sense for the creditor to receive an amount that is at least that net he would receive if he obtained a total victory in court.

Sometimes, when it appears a settlement is possible, to encourage the settlement and avoid the time and rigors of trial, the creditor's attorney will reduce his fee enough, contingent on settlement, to permit settlement.

Insurance Claim

An insurance claim is a hybrid in the matter of fees. It can be a percentage, much as would be any claim or debt sought collected. It can be on a flat fee basis, or on an hourly basis. The variant will depend upon the facts involved.

However, an insurance claim in an automobile case is by custom a percentage. Although the lawsuit is not brought against the insurance company, but against either the other automobile driver or owner, or both, as a practical matter the majority of cases do concern themselves with an insurance company taking over the defense.

The insurance company's attorney is either on a retainer, is employed by the company a salaried attorney, or is retained for each matter by the insurance company on an agreed basis. The basis may be time and this time charge may be different depending on the court concerned. The plaintiff's attorney requires the signing of a retainer agreement. This agreement requires a percentage, up to fifty percent, though sometimes the percentage may be lessened over a certain dollar recovery amount. As the retainer agreement provices for a percentage or recovery, the plaintiff who dismisses his attorney after signing the retainer form, may find himself obligated to pay the percentage whenever and however he recovers.

Traffic Court Problem

The fees in traffic court problems cannot be related to the related to the amount of the potential fine. No attorney can offer his services so cheaply. The attorney retained for these matters must be cognizant that he is asked to serve because the matter is more important than a possible minor dollar fine.

The problem can be one of principal. It can mean that a possible revocation of the right to drive is involved. This in turn can be either personally annoying or be a detriment to the accused's business life. The problem could involve punishment. If an accumulation of offenses are to be tried, then not only a large total dollar fine can be concerned, but also punishment.

In these instances the fee may be on a time basis, or within an estimated range (subject to correction if events show the time and problems so require). A flat fee can be contemplated perhaps if the probable work that should be done is restricted, such as attendance at one hearing, coupled with the necessary preparation for the hearing.

Copyrights, Trademarks and Patents

The fees in these matters relate to what the work is before the attorney. The filing of a copyright application as the filing of a trademark registration application can be on a flat fee. The matter can be intricate and involved and require a time basis. Disbursements in all cases would be additional.

Even the seemingly simple application can involve too much time for the flat fee and a time basis charge would be required.

Contracts involving the licensing of a copyright, a trademark, and a patent would come under the same considerations as other business contracts. Time is the usual factor, with the attorney bearing in mind the value to the client so an overly high time charge is not run up.

The defense of these rights, proprietary rights as called, would be a time basis, as would be offense action against an infringer. In all instances the particular relationship of client and attorney may mean these matters are handled as part of a regular business retainer or some other method not apparently related to either the worth of the task or the type of work performed.

Admiralty

The fees for admiralty work can be said to be a combination of time charges and contingency. In maritime accidents, the factor of success can mean a higher fee. Although there will be a time based charge, if a matter involves a greater sum of money, the fee (if success is had) will be greater than if the sum of money involved is minor. This approach to an attorney's fees is followed regardless if it is the plaintiff or the defendant the attorney represents.

In the drafting of contracts pertaining to maritime matters, time is the basis, with consideration to the worth of the matter involved.

Matrimonial Difficulty

Matrimonial matters are a combination of fee practices. Initially a retainer is requested. Against the hours this retainer would represent, an account is kept. Upon the time spent equalling the amount of retainer paid in, a "refresher" (an additional amount) is requested. Thus, in effect an hourly charge basis is arrived at.

Initially, when the person comes in for consultation, there is a fee request. This fee request in theory could be used up in just discussing if there is a matrimonial problem that could and should be resolved by legal action. It could be that the attorney, finding there is no legal remedy for the problem, or perhaps to put it more accurately, there is no legal remedy that the client is willing to face, will find the matter then concluded. The retainer having been paid in, in all likelihood the matter is ended then as far as the fee situation goes.

In addition to the fee paid by the male of the matrimonial duo, there is the fee paid by the female. This is ultimately the responsibility of the male in most instances. Thus, any arrangements made by the female are those the male must accept.

Tort Action

Tort action can be negligence as customarily understood; that means to most people automobile accidents. Rightly it also includes accidents on or damages to a person's property, and injuries inflicted to a person by any means. In all instances there is a claim seeking to put a dollar value on the injuries, and on the damages to property.

Attorneys for the seeking party, the plaintiff, usually charge a percentage of the recovery. This can be up to one-half of the recovered amount. In some instances court regulations may control the percentage, even requiring a reduction for higher recoveries. In all instances however, a client is asked to sign a retainer agreement. This provides for the percentage to be paid the attorney. Eve if that attorney is dismissed by the plaintiff, the chances are the attorney's right to the percentage recovery may not be impaired.

The charges are made by custom, and although it could be alleged that a better way can be found, the point is a better way has not been found.

The attorneys defending charges based upon tort, negligence of any sort with the dollar claim, are paid either on a regular retainer or volume basis, or per case, or on a time basis. Some have fixed fees on a "per diem" (by day) basis depending on the court concerned. The higher the court, the higher the fee. They are not paid on how much they save over the stated claim. If they were so paid collusion could result with plaintiffs' attorneys. This also would reduce any desire to fight to the last for a complete defensive victory as contrasted to settling early and securing the maximum fees per time invested.

Trial

Trial matters involve two basic elements. The hidden part is the preparation. In effect it compares to an iceberg, the vast bulk being beneath the surface. The showing portion, the peak of all efforts, is the trial itself. Total preparation may be done by the same attorney as appears at the trial; or a minimum of this work may concern his attention.

In any event, the trial portion may command different fees than the preparation, or it can be the same. Some attorneys will charge for trial by the day, or even half-day for more or less routine matters, with hourly or day time charges for the preparation portion. To the extent others are involved in the preparation, or assist at the trial, their charges, while perhaps having the same base as hourly or per diem, may be lesser in base amount. Some attorneys may have other arrangements, including a total charge that will include the work of other attorneys including the actual trial attorney.

After trial the work for the victor is the entering the judgment and execution of it. This may or may not involve additional charges depending upon the time spent. In the collection of a money judgment, additional charges should be expected. (In some metropolitan areas there are attorneys who do nothing else, and their charges are usually a percentage of the amount involved.) The attorney who does this, or retains the collection specialist, may charge hourly, or reflect the percentage charge of the collection specialist if this particular cost is not billed directly.

Arbitration

There is a certain kinship in trial and arbitration fee statements. In both there is the attendance, the out of office, factor. In trail attendance is at a court; in arbitration the hearing can be in an office room. In both the per diem or time basis may be used. In both the preparation for court or hearing can be lengthy and will be usually a time charge. There is nothing to prevent an attorney from charging a flat fee or making other arrangements suitable to his client and himself.

Where trial and arbitration charges are likely to diverge is after the result. In court, with the decision, there are customary things to be done in preparing the judgment and in following through. In arbitration, although statutes provide that an arbitration decision (called an "award") may be "confirmed" (entered) in court as a judgment, usually this is not done. The parties customarily abide by the award without more ado.

But, if an award is entered in court, or if a party objects to the award on the very few statutory grounds that permit an objection, additional fee charges will be made. These may involve time charges, or depending on the particular attorney-client relationship, could be on a flat fee basis for either side or both sides. For example, an attorney might agree to enter an award in court, so it becomes a judgment, for a prestated amount assuming the other side does not contest the matter. A contest might increase the fee.

Arbitration in the usual format does not provide for appeal. The matter is concluded after the hearing, or after possible entry of the award as a judgment (be this directly after the award or after defending against objections to confirming the award). In the few instances where appellate procedure is available, the charges to the client probably will be the same as for court appellate work. This means a time charge, or possibly an agreed upon flat fee.

Criminal Defense

The severity of the crime charged can be the measure of the fees. One noted criminal attorney is alleged to have stated that his fee for a first degree murder charge is all the person has; for that is what the defendant faces. All a person has, in the final analysis, is his life. This can be oversimplified depending on the amount of the person's means, but it illustrates the high cost of criminal defense.

Again, the lower the court in the hierarchy the less are apt to be the fees; this is coupled with the severity of the crime. Generally, fees for criminal work are requested in advance. The reason seems self-evident, for if success alone, total or partial, were the criterion, there could be arguments after the verdict and sentencing as to the right to and amount of the fee.

The charge therefore, is apt to be a flat fee. There is no reason why in lengthy matters per diem charges cannot enter into the arrangements, and frequently they do. But in such instances a retainer with occasional "refreshers" as needed will be sought.

Tax

A tax attorney is a specialist in arguing about money. His fee may vary depending on if it is office and preventive work, or trial and defensive work. The trial aspect, or the hearing aspect (which is akin to a trial but is before an administrative agency) will be on an hourly or a per diem basis. A flat fee can be charged, and most likely will be for less complicated matters or for matters of limited dollar evaluation that will not be pressed beyond a dollar value point to become a matter of principle.

Tax preventive work is on an hourly basis. It is not a percentage of monies saved, although this basis could be a consideration in a particular matter. Generally though, a percentage would not be to a client's advantage. It would not bring forth either the best efforts of the tax attorney or provide the best in accurate service to the client.

Business and Securities

The fee on these two items of business problems can be viewed together. The matter is individual to the circumstances. The amount of work contemplated and performed, the regularity of dealings between the attorney and client, the scope of work usually performed, and the value of the legal work all enter into the size of the fee.

In some particular instances, the fee may be only partially money. In the incorporation of a business, an attorney may be willing to accept his fee or a portion thereof in stocks or notes of the corporation. In the placement of securities to the investing public, an attorney may, again in lieu of all or a portion of a monetary fee, accept securities or rights to buy securities at certain agreed upon prices.

The basis of charge can be time, flat fee, or a percentage, as when securities are placed for purchase by investors. A combination of these methods can be made. There is no set, or customary, basis of charging for legal services. The matter is highly individual, both as to the problem and to the client relationship.

In some instances a general attorney will serve a non-incorporated business, then aid the business in its incorporation. However, when securities are issued for potential outside purchase, a law specialist may be asked to aid. What has been stated before as to fee does not change as to the general business attorney. It can apply also as to the fee of the attorney specializing in the laws of security placement.

To minimize legal fee costs, an attorney may be asked to join the business, as when the business is a corporation, as a director or officer or both. The attorney will be expected to attend to certain legal tasks, or give a certain portion of his time, all as agreed upon beforehand. For this in-businees work the attorney will receive a salary. For work over and above this corporate work, he, or his law firm, will receive fees.

From the attorney's view, this is a good relationship. From the business-view, it solidifies the rapport, for the attorney becomes a vital part of the endeavor. The attorney gains by sharing in the benefits of corporate employees. These benefits can include stock rights and options, profit-sharing, deferred compensation, pension rights, health, life and other insurance benefits. These and other items really cannot be duplicated under our tax laws by a person not employed by a corporation. Because certain of these items are not taxable to the attorney, but would cost him post-tax dollars to duplicate, he gains as does the corporation from this closer relationship.

Retainer

A retainer can be for an individual matter or for a series of matters. In an individual matter charged with high emotion a retainer may be used to insure at least some payment to the attorney. Matrimonial matters and criminal defense are obvious examples. However, even seemingly staid contract involvements can require a retainer. This compensates the attorney at least in part. In addition, a "refresher" can be asked as hourly or per diem charges advance with work.

The series of matters usually is represented by an individual or a business with constant legal needs. Then, depending upon the terms of the retainer, the attorney may serve his client without regard to the value of the items involved; without concern as the kind of work to be performed; and to at least a minimum of time without additional charges to the client. In the largest of matters the retainer can be large enough, and broad enough in scope, to include the handling of any and all matters, in any forum, and of any type, for the client for a set period. In such instances, if the time spent is over the hourly charge that would have resulted, when the retainer next comes up for review, the attorney and client will adjust for the future based on the lessons of the past.

Legal Aid

Legal Aid refers to those societies sponsored by the bar associations usually, or at least starting with an origin of responsible attorneys. It seeks to give legal protection to those unable to carry the cost of private attorney representation. Staff attorneys are on call, and some are aided in addition by volunteers from the roles of privately practising attorneys.

The charges are either minimal, or none, depending upon the individual and the situation. Work in criminal defensive, and in those problems faced by all individuals in the course of life, can be encountered.

Legal Aid is supported by charitable contributions from private sources usually.

There are other organizations and groups which seek to aid those without funds or adequate funds. The government and bar associations have sponsored groups of attorneys to serve on a volunteer basis in "store-front" legal offices, taking whatever problems arise. There is currently an evolving controversy as to whether or not organizations or unions can provide general legal services to members. These services would be on a minimal cost or no cost basis; they would be from a staff of attorneys or be performed by an attorney of the individual's choice.

In all instances there is always the question of what is proper low or no cost aid and what should be the fee-basis. Today this is undergoing change. Before it seemed as though the low or no cost aid involved defensive matters. Now it seems this is not so, but can involve the beginning creation of business endeavors. These businesses, if successful, could grow financially and require private attorney representation.

For whom a form of legal aid should be made available is an open question. Sometimes an income statement, coupled with an evaluation of a person's capital resources, determines if such aid will be available to the individual. In other organizations and groups, the criterion for aid may be membership in the particular group. "Membership" in such instances does not mean a formal joining, but an identity usually one of neighborhood or other evident oneness with the group. For aid by unions and other organizations, the criterion would be the formal membership in the union or other organization.

General Considerations

In all relationships with an attorney, the client should not hesitate to inquire as to fees. An attorney cannot state accurately what these will be unless it is a flat fee or percentage basis. Much of the cost can depend on the client demands for time. A constant request for advice; a constant telephoning; and a need for repetitive aid takes an attorney's time and reflects itself in increased billings.

On the other hand, a letter from an attorney to the client confirming their discussion is not necessarily an additional cost to the client. If the attorney does not write and confirm, he would instead usually prepare a file memorandum; and this would have a cost without an advantage. The advantage is what should be self-evident: the client knows what the attorney believes was discussed and the client then has a chance to make any necessary corrections before matters have proceeded too far. Additionally, an attorney seeking to best serve his client may send copies of letters received or sent from time to time on the client's matter, or just inform the client of no progress. This is not a waste, but is in the scope of things, a matter of good service. Again, the client is kept abreast of matters and has the opportunity to comment before matters have gone too far.

Some clients may prefer to entrust everything to the attorney and not have communiques of any sort, relying on the attorney to advise when a matter is completed. This complete delegation is not for the average person, and seemingly should be utilized only by a person who has benefited from the particular attorney's services before with satisfactory results. Further, the client should recognize that in whatever statement for professional services he receives there can be amounts of work that have no way of appearing as done except by faith. Thus, the necessity for the rapport noted earlier in this book.

Clients may anticipate that a problem is simple of statement and simple of solution, but find the attorneys spends time. To the legal view things are not usually black and white, but are cast in many varying shades of grey. With the grey predominant, inquiries and work requiring time must be spent. Time equals a charge. In essence, if a satisfactory attorney has been retained, he will do what work is necessary and will try to explain if asked.

In sum, a candid and open exchange between attorney and client should be sought and achieved.

Expenditures

An attorney's expenditures on behalf of his client constitute a separate item for the client to pay. These charges are additional to the fee, or professional service charge.

Some attorneys include within the fee statement and without itemization all expenditures or disbursements they encounter. These attorneys prefer to calculate their fees with such items in mind. At the other extreme, some attorneys will bill each and every item, including a predetermined rate for local telephone calls and a per line stenographic cost. Some attorneys will mix fee and disbursement billings. One attorney, when he had a luncheon conference with his client, determined his particular charge by who paid the luncheon check. If the client did, his charge was less than if he, the attorney, paid the check. This is not to say it is an approved practice.

Generally, the attorney will bill for all large expenditures. These might include items such as court and other governmental filing fees, court stenographic charges, and appraisals. In the case of wills, where only a nominal fee is charged by many attorneys, a proportionate stenographic cost is not unusual. Other attorneys will keep a record of each item that is directly attributable to serving a client, recognizing that even the matter of regular postage becomes a sizeable sum over a period of time.

What practice is followed in any matter is for the attorney concerned to decide. His client may inquire as to the procedure the particular attorney follows, but the client cannot expect the procedure to be changed unless a compensating fee adjustment is made. And, the attorney may not be willing to change a general office bookkeeping practice to accommodate one client or one matter. This should be understood by the client.

In some matters, where the attorney is to bill the client for his professional services upon conclusion of the matter, or at some predetermined regular interval, disbursement statements may be submitted either in advance or upon reaching a certain sum in outlays. There is no regular practice on this, but is an individual consideration. With a new client an attorney might be more apt to request an advance against disbursements than with a client with whom a billing and payment pattern is known.

Chapter V

LOCATING AN ATTORNEY

Securing an attorney can be haphazard or the result of careful inquiry and search. Life is such that there is a degree of the uncertain in all endeavors, but to the extent some choice is possible, it should be made.

Finding an attorney is not a matter of going down the street, looking at signs, or picking up a telephone book or other directory, and then stopping in. The attorney, as a doctor, handles a client-patient's life. In criminal matters the literal nature of this statement is evident. It is just as accurate as other items. In wills, the client's entire life's work, as displayed by material possessions, is dependent on the attorney's writing. In business contracts, the gain or loss, an economic life or death, can be affected by the attorney's work.

Thus, where to find an attorney is a more serious problem than the average person does believe. The fact that someone known to the individual is an attorney, be that person a friend, relative, or acquaintenace, does not by itself, answer the quest for legal assistance.

Directories

There are several sources that constitute this term "directories."

The Classified [Yellow] Pages: No one should utilize this method for selection of an·attorney. The listing is for address and telephone confirmation. There can be no other purpose of worth, other than to confirm name spelling.

Martindale-Hubbell Law Directory: This is a general directory, attempting to list every attorney now practicing in the United States, or for a United States law firm abroad.

The arrangement is by states, subdivided into cities, with that area's attorneys listed alphabetically. The year of birth and year of admission to the Bar are noted, followed by code numbers for the college and law school attended. The code is explained in the front of the volume. Before each attorney's name, if he is a member of the American Bar Association, is a triangle symbol. The fact of membership is not evidence of professional skill by and of itself. A rating is present, "a v" being the highest possible to receive. This rating is obtained after ten years legal practice if the attorney's peers, then bearing the same rating, agree. Before the ten year period, but after five years, a "b" can be had. The rating applies only as to a particular locale. Therefore, if an attorney has offices in more than one state, it is necessary to consult under the listing of his principal office.

The bulk of each volume is made up of professional cards as they are called. These cards can be inserted only by a law firm with the "a v" rating or by an individual attorney with this rating. If one partner in a law firm has the "a v" rating, the law firm can insert a professional card. If one is interested in a particular individual, his inquiry should be as to the rating carried by that individual, and not by his firm. A biographical sketch is inserted here. Some sketches are more complete than are others, but all expand on the basic information set forth in the forefront of the book.

This directory can be used to find the statistical type of information (years and schools) but it shows in the professional card section in what fields the attorney, or his law firm, believes competence lies, and also what the attorney has done or represents. The reference work, now with 4 of its 5 volumes, all of very thin and many pages, devoted to attorney listings, is prepared for attorney libraries. Some larger general libraries have copies. If not, a courthouse law library probably has the set and the work can be viewed there.

Law Lists: There are many of these, some claiming a listing of attornys specializing in certain areas of law practice, and others with other claims of competence. The American Bar Association passes on all lists under standards its committee administers. In spite of this however, these lists cannot be compared in usefulness with the Martindale-Hubbell listing.

Social, fraternal, and other lists: Some organizations publish lists of members, even attractive booklets, noting home and business addresses. The business affiliation is noted, and so is the professional sphere. Unless a person is seeking someone previously known, or believes a choice should be made because of the kinship of belonging, that is, a mutual affiliation, these lists are akin to a telephone classified direction in usefulness.

Family Attorney

In some families a family attorney is a part of the domestic scene. The choice of this person, or firm of attorneys, to serve the individual's needs comes logically to the fore. Yet, this could be a disservice to the attorney as well as to the individual.

If the attorney has been accustomed to handle problems of the family, it is likely he looks to the head of the family for guidance. Probably he has seen, and does see matters with this guide consciously or subconsciously steering him.

There can be matters that the individual would embark upon that do not fit into the family pattern. There could be differences of opinion. These need not be dramatic and difficult breaks with family solidarity, but can require independent counsel for the client's own peace of mind. Because of these situations, independent counsel should be considered.

On the other hand, continuation of the family attorney or firm for a family business could be sagacious. There, a continuing knowledge of the situations faced before could serve as an aid that cannot be duplicated readily by new counsel. This assumes, of course, satisfaction and a rapport has been achieved between the attorney and the individual now dealing with the attorney.

Corporation Attorney

In many corporations, the attorney handling the corporation's legal affairs is sought by the employees for the handling of individual legal problems. This can be whether or not the corporate attorney is a corporation employee (a salaried attorney) or he is in a law firm that serves the corporation.

If the corporation attorney is salaried, it seems the work he might perform for an individual must be supplementary to the work his salary requires. The work he does for the individual might be done after business hours, or inbetween other tasks. If the corporate attorney is an outside attorney, being a member or associate of the corporation's law firm, the client relationship is clearer. In both instances, however, for the purposes of this section, the wisdom of his selection is at issue.

The attorneys who serve a persons' pl ∘ of business, unless the individual owns the business, are not likely to be best for all matters. If a continuing attorney-client relationship is to be established, this can be a weakness. At some time the individual may have a problem concerning his employment with the corporation. An example may be his rights as an employee or his rights under a pension program. In these situations the attorney's first obligation will be to his business client, and to that extent he must disqualify himself from handling the individual's problems. No attorney can serve both sides as a general rule. Thus, in choosing the corporate attorney there is the danger, even the possibility, that the individual will be limiting himself as to the full-coverage of legal services he can received. Also, although the client relationship must be preserved, sometimes the corporate attorney does continue in the corporation on a non-legal level, advancing to a position where the individual's job performance is subject to his approval. In such situations, it seems reasonable to assume that the former attorney, being human, may consciously or not recall any difficulty between corporation and individual, thereby hindering the individual's advancement or even business continuation.

74

Further, if the business situation is such that the business attorney believes or feels obligated to handle some employee affairs, even at a relatively token fee, this cannot lay a basis for a continuing relationship. If the business connection is severed, the attorney will no longer have this rationale or emotional obligation to continue.

Individuals

Each individual has his own set of preferences, or prejudices. An individual may have different expectations of those with whom he works and as to those served by him and finally as to those who serve him. With this caveat, inquiry of those who have been served by attorneys can be fruitful. The question should be adequacy of service, and the fee the secondary question. To some the professional service given may be deemed excellent but at a high fee, to others the service may be criticized while accepting the fee as reasonable; yet for both the work and the fee can be the same. The people viewing it provide the difference. The question of capability is the important one. Although it may be difficult for an individual to know capability, nevertheless an opinion will be formed of the attorney's capability. For similar work, one person may believe the work deserves high praise and another accept it as expected routine, without perhaps perceiving the depth of thought that went into its doing. Talking about this can help. The inquirer will form impressions.

What it may come down to is the relationship the individuals bear to the other, the inquirer to the listener. If the relationship or friendship is one originating over business-dealings that are on a continuing basis, this means that if a business dispute arose, no matter how amicable the parties remain each to the other, the attorney could not counsel both parties. Thus, the need for legal counsel would be limited in its realization.

If the friendship is social, the likelihood of independent legal needs is lessened substantially.

In using another's attorney it may be advisable not to tell the other either about the reason for the visitation or of the continuing need. The attorney will keep his counsel, but if by any chance he should not, he can and should be chastened.

Inquiry of individuals who have not used an attorney still can be of aid. Sometimes an individual may have knowledge both of things and people that others lack. A contact may be suggested that would be helpful.

Religious Sources

Meeting at, or finding a recommendation from an individual's religious house was a more regular source than it is today. Church attendance is not an equation of legal ability. Lawyers are as people, and if Lincoln were to have relied on church contacts for his clients when he was an attorney, he might have fared poorly in his law practice.

In past times when religious attendance was a more compulsive matter, the church would have been a usual place to make acquaintance of those with whom an individual would deal. There is the saying that the "law is a jealous mistress." The attorney may have worked not only the five day week, but Saturday as well. Sunday may be his only day for his family or other recreation and he may not choose to spend the day in formal religious contemplation. This is not a commentary as to value, but a statement of fact that finds its parallel with persons of many occupations.

To the extent a client's problems may have religious preferences or implications, an attorney at least sympathetic to the individual's beliefs may be welcomed. Then, an attorney either known to be of the same persuasion, met in a religious context, or recommended by an individual known there, might serve well.

Accountant

More people may use accountants than use attorneys. At least tax questions arise yearly, and so an acquaintance can be regular. To the extent the accountant used is respected his opinion may be helpful. The accountant probably can introduce the individual to several attorneys, giving the individual a choice. This is not to imply that the accountant's recommendation is to be taken as an absolute, but to note that it is a start or possible point of departure.

If the accountant is also an attorney, the individual should decide in what capacity he prefers service. The problems of law and accounting have overlapping areas. The thought process, and value judgments, entering into each can vary immensely. Further, there can be times when the legal advice sought can be at variance with the accounting needs of the client. Both views can be client resolved, and not by another handling both functions. Still more to the point of separation, a separate relationship can aid in full service. The accountant, if serving as the individual's attorney may be reluctant to stress additional accounting work needs for fear of seeming to produce work. An attorney would not be so burdened. The reverse is logical also. A separate role may cause each to suggest, or to deny, work that properly is judged by client needs alone.

Banks

A bank cannot recommend attorneys. It can note the attorney the bank uses. Most probably these attorneys are competent for the bank work, but this does not mean they would be suitable for an individual's problems. At certain times a conflict, even though it is not realized consciously by the attorney, can arise. For example, if the individual is seeking advice on the drafting of a will, it would be illogical to expect the attorney who serves the bank as well not to favor the bank for fiduciary positions concerned.

On the other hand, the individual bank officer, as an individual who meets people, may be of aid. To the extent he can and does speak as an individual or friend, he can aid as would any individual.

Clubs

The term "clubs" includes professional, social, and political organizations. These are forums for meeting people most assuredly. A certain bond, no matter how tenuous it can reveal itself to be, is shown by the common demoninator of the same club. A social club offers an opportunity to see the attorney under somewhat relaxed circumstances, and perhaps gain an impression of his human worth.

Political clubs have spawned the "club-house politician." This is a derogatory term used for certain persons, sometimes attorneys, who frequent a local-level political club. Perhaps in the main these persons have a forte other than law, but within a political club there can be budding statesmen, lawyers with civic zeal, and of all ages, and careful practitioners of law with some pseudo-political ambitions as well as attorneys seeking political appointments from the particular party's judges or courthouse organization. While an attorney's political ambitions are to be encouraged, a basic question is whether or not the attorney is practicing law as a primary goal or practicing politics with law as a means of temporary survival. Civil interest by an attorney as with any other individual is applauded. To the extent the attorney's motivation is civic, and law is his primary motivation, service can be primary for the client. Here the meeting ground affords an opportunity to estimate the attorney as an individual and make an appraisal of his worth.

There can be clubs devoted to a person's work as well. Professional groups such as attorneys' bar associations come to mind. There can be other groups such as teacher's groups, as some attorneys may teach a course or two in local community colleges. Again, the meeting ground is provided.

Union or fraternal group: Changes are on the horizon as to the propriety of unions and akin organizations to establish legal aid services for their members. These services will be offered either as a part of the union or fraternal dues, or be on a charge basis that may or may not be the charge an individual normally would pay. The selection of the attorney, while not made by the union or fraternal group, may be from those

78

retained by it. Now, this avenue is not the reason for inclusion. To the extent there is a meeting of motives, it may be easier for the individual to find a rapport with an attorney.

An attorney who is associated with a fraternal group, which is a more social-type of organization, will have at least a common denominator with the individual. To the extent this is an aid, the attorney can be questioned as to his professional emphasis.

Doctors and dentists: A person's doctor or dentist is competent presumably to handle medical or dental ailments. Only as an individual are referrals to be valued.

Established Law Firms

Individuals and law firms can be established in the sense of having a community reputation of worth. This topic now refers particularly to the law firm that has a continuity of generations behind its existence. In some instances the names of the partners bear no resemblance to the law firm name.

No law firm can be long established without having good reason for its continuance. A law firm can be changing in character without its perception being noticed by the individual or even by the community. Large office space with less than the number needed to fill it, and bearing a mark of age, shows a lessening standing in the community according to some viewers. The same space with contemporary brightness and the same number of attorneys and aids to fill the space impresses a viewer with optimism for the future. An intangible to judge by assuredly, but nevertheless a very human one.

The law firm should be selected not solely because of its age or competence for old established clients. If its name is valued, the acquisition of new clients is more relevant. Old clients can remain by inertia, the corporation law firm intertwining, inability to change by the corporation without a major discussion, whereas a new client comes because the law firm is offering something. If that something is what is needed by the inquiring individual for himself or his business, then that law firm should be considered.

In essence, while age is of help, the primary judgment of the law firm, as for an individual attorney, is the service that can best aid the individual.

Bar Referral

Bar associations are those law groups to which attorneys belong by voluntary persuasion, or because the particular state in which they practice requires membership as a condition of practicing law. The bar associations may have a committee, or persons, designated to deal with individual law inquiries. These committees or persons have as their function the referring of individuals needing legal advice to attorneys thought capable of handling the problem. An individual inquiring for an attorney to handle a certain type of problem will be referred to a choice of attorneys, or given the name of an attorney thought competent in the field of law needed.

These names can be a good source, but as with any reference, the need is that of the individual. The attorneys referred will be those known to the committee or designated persons handling referral work, and in no way implies other attorneys cannot do as good a task, or perhaps even a superior one. After all, particularly where there are many attorneys, not all can be known to even the most active of bar associations.

With a name, or names, the problem is for the inquirer to see if a rapport is established with the attorney. If it is, the committee's work has been successful, but if a rapport is not found, this does not mean the reverse, that the committee has failed. For a rapport is a personal factor, incapable of being set down in guide-lines for a committee to follow.

Miscellaneous

Other sources can come to mind depending upon the attorney-knowledge and skills needed.

If a criminal attorney is needed, and in haste, the solution to the problem is different than the deliberate search for a business-law oriented attorney.

In a criminal matter, even if the individual knows only a civil attorney, the civil attorney should be contacted. The request then would be for the civil attorney's assistance in retaining a competent criminal attorney. This would be a working together, unless the relationship between the attorney and the individual were so well established that this responsibility would be borne completely by the civil attorney.

If a civil attorney is not known, or if other reasons suggest he should not be consulted, then the individual must seek legal aid on his own. A friend on the police force may tell what attorneys regularly are known to practice in the criminal court. Perhaps a commentary as to ability of the several attorneys can be obtained. A former Federal Bureau of Investigation man can be of service perhaps. A local Legal Aid bureau while not being willing, or permitted, to undertake a matter for an individual with ability to pay, may advise which of its attorneys have opened offices and specialize in the handling of criminal matters.

The bar referral services should not be overlooked, though obviously this is a more leisurely procedure than a midnight call in a criminal matter.

Any attorney willing to make an appearance in a criminal matter while the search for regular counsel goes on can be of aid. However, in fairness to the civil law attorney who is office-oriented, the standards of knowledge and performance cannot be expected to be that of the criminal law devotee. A more than adequate "stop-gap" may be found in use of such an attorney however.

In the search for civil law attorney aid, the casual meeting in an elevator, at any affair, social or business, should not be overlooked. No matter how an attorney is met, the important matter is that he is met and an opinion formed. First impressions to some people are all important; to others they are suspect. But, an impression must be obtained. Therefore, in all instances the meeting of attorney and potential/possible client is most important. All that has gone before suggests possible avenues of introduction to a meeting. Thereafter, because of the extremely personal relationship that should be found between a client and his attorney, the rapport is the important element.

The Basis of Selection

After all is said and done, basically the individual must have a rapport with the attorney. From whatever souce names are given, be it from friends, church or fraternal connections, even enemies whose attorneys have guided them successfully, the inquirer should learn something about the attorney.

He might check the Martindale-Hubbell listing. This is an open book, so to speak, and should offer aid to knowing something about the attorney and his claims of competence.

He should meet the attorney. If he can meet him casually, through a friend arranging a luncheon, even using some excuse other than the real reason, this might be the easiest way. Then, he must talk to the attorney about his dilemma.

Meeting the Attorney

Meeting the attorney is not the same as meeting "your attorney." In the first meeting there should be no question but that an attorney-client relationship is not established unless, and until, both parties wish this to be.

In any relationship there must be certain elements. "Rapport" is a word that can, and does, characterize many aspects. Rapport includes a relation of trust, harmony, conformity, accord, or affinity. It is nebulous, vague, and uncertain; but when it is had, it is felt and known. Without it, there is nothing. This is an emotional response, upon which rationalizations are built. If this is had, at least as far as the would-be client is concerned, then with the attorney's concurrence, the relationship can be established.

Rationalization of what makes a "rapport" can be made. One aspect would be the much-used and much-abused term of these times, "sincerity." An attorney should be believable. Far preferable is an attorney who admits, candidly, that he does not know the answer to the problem posed. Basically, attorneys are not the font of all knowledge. Although law is, proudly and with justice, the "learned profession," the attorney's skill is knowing where to find the answers. Sincerity embraces a willingness to work for the client, in the client's interests; in a sense as though this were the prime task of the attorney's doing.

Time availability is a factor. Although a client must expect to pay for an attorney's time, and time is basically the tool of the attorney, the attorney should be willing and able to give time. If the attorney is too busy, if the matter is *beyond his financial adjustment,* or if he is *not interested sufficiently,* or *any other reason* prohibits his spending reimburseable time, a search elsewhere might be advisable.

The last sentence may be noted. "Too busy" should be self-evident. Some people surround themselves with work beyond that which they can capably do. There are so many hours of work in each week, and if too much is scheduled, a proper devotion to the task cannot be given.

"Beyond his financial adjustment" refers to the matter of overhead. An attorney responsible for heavy overhead, in theory at least, should have greater financial demands upon him, which are in turn, transferred to clients. This is not to say that an attorney with a lesser overhead should be "cheap," for no attorney should be expected to give less-than-worth advice except for clients he serves on what might be termed a "private charitable basis." This is to note that some attorneys cannot, by reason of their overhead costs, handle matters not worth at least a certain minimum in fees. The reference to "private charitable basis" refers to those clients who are not paying full value for the legal services received. Many attorneys have some clients who are not affluent, and they are served by the attorney in the expectation that success will come to them, or because the attorney believes in the client's cause, or because a friend sent the client, or the client is a friend for whom the attorney feels responsible.

"Not interested sufficiently" refers to matters which the attorney finds routine, boring, or not in his special field of interest. Sometimes an attorney will accommodate his client and do a fine task on such work; but it is human to expect that an attorney will do better work when the matter appeals to him than when the matter lacks interest.

"Any other reason" is to open the vast realm of whatever it might be that could prevent proper devotion to a client's affairs. This can be either a personal non-attraction to the would-be client or his matter, or some ambition by the attorney which would conflict with proper attention to the client's problem. "Any other reason" is ethereal, but should be sensed by the client.

In meeting the attorney, the problem is presented, and a relationship is sought. If the time availablility factor seems present, and there is trust established, then somehow the client must seek out an answer to the competence of the particular attorney for the particular problem. Ability to do certain legal matters extremely well is not a criterion of effective handling of other matters. Some attorneys can plan strategy well, understand the legal issues brilliantly, but cannot do court-room work. The attorney who recognizes his limitations, or tries to recognize them, is more apt to be an abler attorney than another attorney without self-imposed boundaries.

The fact that the attorney has no previous experience with an identical problem does not imply inadequacy. No two problems are alike, generally speaking, and no two approaches to the same problem would be akin in all likelihood. The problem should be one that the attorney believes he is competent to handle. This is basically his decision, and returns the evaluation to the factor of trust.

In meeting the attorney, the problem should be presented concisely and clearly. To the extent the problem can be thought out ahead of the visit to the attorney's office, time should be taken in this endeavor. Even an outline might be prepared to which reference can be made as necessary. Most emphatically, all facts surrounding the problem should be given. One function of an attorney is to separate the important from the non-important. What may seem minor, and not worth taking time to relate, can be a salient factor in law. Without knowledge of this point, the answer to the presented problem cannot be complete nor accurate.

The attorney having received the problem should advise what he can and will do. This can be something requiring immediate action, or it can be the seemingly-vague, but necessary, step of taking the matter under advisement.

The fee factor can be raised either then, or at the beginning of the meeting. With some attorneys an initial interview will have a flat fee, which is applied to the total fee that will be owed if work is undertaken. If the attorney is to proceed, the attorney may be able to give an estimate of the range of likely charges, or the basis upon which costs will be computed.

If at the meeting, at any time, the person searching for any attorney does not believe the particular attorney would be proper, the meeting should be terminated.

To some a termination when the other party is present is too terrifying to face. In such instances, immediately after the meeting, a simple letter, enclosing the interview fee if not previously paid, should be sent the attorney. It need offer no reason, but state that the attorney-client relationship will not be. Thus "Please do not proceed upon the matter discussed" is sufficient in all respects from a client's view. An attorney, on the other hand, has certain professional obligations that do not permit such bluntness.

A Client's Obligations to an Attorney

A client, upon becoming that, has a prime obligation, to the attorney. This is complete and absolute honesty. The attorney cannot represent the client adequately if items are held back that could be pertinent to the matter. The attorney is the proper judge of this.

An analogy to the medical doctor is apt. The doctor must know all health factors to try and heal. The doctor of law (and this degree is coming into increasing prominence) must know all economic and factual details surrounding the particular legal problem to be of assistance.

The client has the obligation to pay the attorney promptly. This seemingly self-evident statement would not be made if the facts showed its observation was a regular practice. If there is a question as to a fee, the client has a right and should ask the attorney the basis for the charge.

The client has the obligation to the attorney to respond to questions asked, secure papers needed, keep appointments, and generally cooperate. The problems usually put to an attorney cannot be resolved without further client participation. If they can be, and the client does not wish to know anything but the result, receiving no progress reports, then the client should so inform the attorney. But in the average matter cooperation will be necessary. Although the attorney is retained ["hired" is not the proper verb] to represent the client, a failure to be prompt with cooperation cannot aid the client's cause. Not only is the attorney human, but at some point duplicating requests for information must bear a time charge that the client should expect to pay.

Double Clients and Ethics

An attorney is held to rigorous standards by the Code of Professional Responsibility. Among the canons of ethics, all prepared by the American Bar Association, is one headed "A lawyer should exercise independent professional judgment on behalf of a client." This particular canon states that the attorney exercises his work "solely for the benefit of his client and free of compromising influences and loyalties. Neither his personal interests, the interests of other clients, nor the desires of third persons should be permitted to dilute his loyalty to his client."

This means that when an attorney is retained by one person, he cannot represent another person that might have differing interests. Even in a so-termed "friendly transaction," generally the attorney should not represent both the buyer and the seller, and sometimes not even co-buyers nor co-sellers. If the attorney represents a group, he should not represent someone seeking something from that group. For example, a school board attorney should not represent an aggrieved person

86

before that school board. The fact that the attorney concerned is the only one in the immediate locale is not of moment. There are other attorneys, from separate law offices, that can be called in from a nearby area.

There are exceptions to multiple representation, but these require full disclosure by the attorney to each client. Even then the attorney can continue the multi-representation only if all the clients consent. This consent must be had on each occasion the question arises. The attorney cannot seek to obtain a blanket endorsement before each issue arises.

The attorney may represent multi-clients not having differing interests. Sometimes, but not always, co-beneficiaries under a will are such persons. But, the attorney must explain any circumstances that could cause a question to arise. If a client questions the attorney's ability to represent more than one client, the attorney must defer and cease representation of that client.

The attorney also is bound not to promote his own self interest to a client. This includes the naming of the attorney as the executor or trustee of his client's instrument. This is not to say the attorney cannot serve; it is to say the attorney should not push for such appointment.

An attorney retained by a corporation, or other legal entity, represents it and not the individual who may be a part (no matter how vital) of it. The attorney may serve the individual on a non-conflicting matter; but not when the individual and corporate interests might clash.

In general, the legal profession seeks to insure that an attorney serves well and with undivided loyalty. The profession believes that only in this way can the client receive the legal representation to which he is entitled.

Chapter VI

SUGGESTIONS TO HELP OBTAIN
MORE EFFICIENT LEGAL SERVICE

The obtaining of more efficient legal service is a justifiable self-centered goal. Efficient legal services means more is obtained per legal fee dollar spent. More prompt legal service should result from helping to make possible the obtaining of efficient legal service.

The client can contribute to this efficient goal. The client can prepare for discussion with the attorney. He can, and should outline his problem at least mentally, and if he can, even make an outline on paper. This is helpful particularly if complicated facts are involved. If specifications or details are concerned, the client should have these ready for review.

The client should gather together, and keep, records and papers as they should be kept, or as they can be maintained more helpfully. This means that information can be obtained more quickly, and so more efficiently. If this is not done, a jumble may be given to the attorney for his sorting prior to reading and thought.

The efficiency goal is a cooperative venture, and means a client gain. The attorney, if freed from detail at least as to a particular client's matter, can approach the matter with fresh verve. Chargeable time in detail clearing will not be needed, and this can mean possibly more rapid answers and a lower fee paid by the client.

Consideration of the attorney's time is required. A telephone call or a visit for no reasonably discernible reason logically results in either time charges or efficiency lowering. On the other hand, failure to communicate developments to an attorney on events touching on the matter before him, could mean wasted legal time is spent. "Common sense" (and common sense is a term of art admittedly) must be used. The client should not attempt to eliminate records, for the attorney must review all to determine what is pertinent; nor must the client seek to not communicate events. But, if the client can present papers and developments to the attorney in an orderly manner, the client should gain.

Efficiency is a relative thing, particularly in anything as subjective as the human mind. An attorney may find the solution, the approach to success, to a client's problem when he is out of his office and is not consciously dwelling on the problem. The efficient use of an attorney's powers does not mean office time alone. It means the use of an attorney's time, both in office and out, so that his best efforts can be given when in the office, and his entire being can be relaxed sufficiently to contribute solutions to problems facing him.

A famous entrepreneur, when questioned about a highly paid executive who seemed to spend much time gazing out of the window, remarked that he would hire many others just like the gazer if they too could come up with the varied ideas of great value as did the window-gazing executive.

So it is with an attorney, or anyone for whom thought processes are so important. The place where, and the atmosphere within which problem-solving can be related, may not be only the office. The attorney must be freed from routine bogging detail to the extent possible. In greater measure this is up to the attorney himself to do, but as touched upon above, in many ways a client can contribute a great deal.

Records to Keep

More and more, as life becomes a matter of history, it is necessary to keep records. Records can relate to general as well as specific matters in and of a person's life. Records can refer to matters unrelated to the need for an attorney, or they can be such that might be useful when consulting an attorney.

Tax records are the thought of many people as the most important records for retention. Some believe tax returns, as filed, should be kept as long as the person lives. Other persons suggest ten years is adequate. The keeping of the supporting papers, the bills and receipts, the payment records, and so on, that went into the preparation of the tax returns are another matter. Safety indicates these should be kept a minimum of six years. If possible, stretch this to ten years. If any tax return was audited, or there was a tax hearing at the minimum, the papers supporting successive tax years, as well as the returns, should be kept indefinitely.

Records include valuable papers. The two are not necessarily synonymous. A birth certificate, christening, baptismal or other religious certificate, marriage certificate (if issued), evidence of matrimonial changes, children's birth certificates, armed service release, cemetary lot ownership, and death certificates of immediate family members are valuable papers. Yet, except in unusual circumstances, all can be replaced by an application and fee paid to the appropriate office. Noting when, where and what each stated paper represents constitutes a record. Such a record should be kept.

In addition, all life changes should be noted. These would include business and professional memberships, social memberships, awards and honors received, a chronology of schooling, jobs and description, citizenship if applicable, and various items as to armed and other government service.

Life changes requires noting the important events in life with some detail, and noting where supporting proof can be obtained if this pertinent. Related information should be given. For example, as to marriage, the date, place, and full name of a person's spouse come to mind. If a marriage was terminated, details should be noted. The record made should note where any additional information can be found as well as the location of official documentation.

The names, birth dates and places, and present addresses of close relatives, such as parents, brothers and sisters should be noted, as well as the same for a person's children. If a person's children are married, the date, place of marriage and to whom should be set down, along with the current addresses. For deceased family members noting where they are buried may be useful. Much of this is information as was kept in old family Bibles, but the suggested record goes further.

If a Power of Attorney was given to anyone, that person's name and address, as well as noting the scope of the Power given, should be noted.

If a person has served in the armed services there are additional records needed. Service dates and position, retired pay or other benefits should be set down. As befits the individual situation, details should be given. Some benefits may survive the payee's death and be paid to a spouse or another. If there is a specific bureau that should be notified, this should be named.

Additionally, there should be a listing of places where valuable papers and records are kept. To the extent combination local numbers must be given, or the location of a key to a safe or safe deposit box is set down, the listing should be restricted. It can be given to a trusted friend, the person's attorney, or another. Some recipients may prefer to receive this information in a sealed envelop, and this can be done as the parties wish.

Papers to Keep

The papers behind the records just noted, or the papers which make up the record, if had, should be kept. These papers should be kept carefully, preferably in a fire-proof box. A safe-deposit bank box is not essential. The reason for keeping papers, if already in hand, is that duplication takes time and could mean delay at an inconvenient time.

There are certain definite papers which should be kept. A summary, or record, might be kept, depending on the individual matter.

On any time payment, such as a mortgage, a running account is given the payor in the form of a certificate or paper each pay period. This lists the amount paid, due, and when. Certainly the last paper should be kept, being replaced each time with the next one. Similar papers would be any charge account monthly statement. A notation on the last paper kept of when the amount said due was paid, and the check number can be helpful if a question arises.

Bank statements, and the checks returned along with the depositor's copy of deposits made, should be retained as tax return evidence. Auditing of a person's tax return requires production of bank books and records to see if any unusually large deposits or withdrawal has been made. Therefore, it might seem these statements should be kept only for the six year minimum noted earlier. Other uses for these bank statements, as well as other papers and records showing the reason for deposits or withdrawal, may mean the papers should be kept a longer period of time. For example, some checks, or other papers and records, may be evidence of a contract being paid, or not paid. They might support a basis of a capital addition to property, which would be treated in a different way than a casual expenditure of minor amounts. This is, or can be important for reasons of taxation or sale price many years later.

The Statute of Limitations is a term that refers to that period of time within which a dispute may be brought by legal means. In some states, after one or two years, any agreement that was not written cannot be enforced in court by an aggrieved party. In some states a written contract must be enforced within six years.

In addition to the Statute of Limitations there is a concept called waiver and another called estoppel. In essence, these terms refer to particular facts whereby a complaining party is prohibited from enforcing a contract. For example, one person may have acted in such a way the defending party thought the matter was ended. The term estoppel also refers to the behavior of a party. Because of something the person has done, he is estopped (prevented) from changing his course of behavior. This could mean one person is prevented from enforcing the contract, or the other person is prevented from denying the contract's validity.

A person should not rely entirely on the Statute of Limitations of his particular state. The reason is that another state may have a different, and longer period of time. Unless there is an absolute certainty that a particular state law governs, it might be risky to throw out papers relying on his state's Statute of Limitations.

There is another concept that must be noted. This concerns a court judgment. If a court has decided in favor of a party, that person can enfore the judgment. Usually a judgment has a long Statute of Limitations, running about twenty years in some states.

With such time considerations, the immediate reaction is to keep all papers for all time. As a practical matter this is awkward if not impossible.

In great part, a practical solution is to throw away papers, and receipts, after the sixth year of keeping. But, if the paper refers to an amount that is large to the individual, keep the paper for a longer period of time. For example, if the last particular department store monthly statement is six years old, it need not be kept; but if a dispute was settled involving several months income and a paper was signed evidencing this, probably the safest thing would be to keep the paper at least ten years. The reason is that an individual might not be able to afford the chance of losing this amount.

Contracts or memoranda relating to contracts that have not been completed and contracts with which some dissatisfaction was expressed should be kept until nothing can be done about the matter.

Some papers could conceivably be used throughout a person's life. These might include copies of recommendations by persons concerning employment held or sought, a copy of a job resume, and copies of applications for positions or memberships. These and other items may have a reference value, however nebulous it may seem at the moment, and should be kept indefinitely.

Numerical Identification

Numerical identification is a potential aid to the individual and to his family in life, and after death to those surviving him.

In addition to an individual's Social Security number and armed services identification number, an individual frequently has other numbers. These can include the numbers for each bank account, savings, checking and safe deposit box, each stock or commodity brokerage account, driver's license, gasoline credit cards, general charge or credit cards, individual store charge accounts, club memberships, health insurance memberships, life and other insurance policies.

In some instances these numbers are impressed on plastic cards, used by the individual in credit transactions. In other cases, the number is a means of identification that appears in a record book, and can be helpful although not essential to benefits.

For credit cards, a loss can impose a financial risk. A finder of a lost card, or a person stealing a credit card can use it. Depending on the terms of the agreement with the card issuing company, the individual may be responsible until the company has notification. A list of number identification should be prepared, kept current, and duplicated.

A responsible family member as well as the individual should know where a copy of the numerical listing is kept. Another person, such as the individual's attorney (if he has a regular attorney-client relationship) also might have a copy. If the individual loses his wallet containing his credit cards, for example, and even if he is away from his home or office, a telephone call to his family or attorney can summon valuable aid. The person called quickly can notify the card-issuing companies. By giving the person's name and identification number, rapid steps to protect the individual from unauthorized charges can be made. This in turn may facilitate the individual's reissuance of credit facilities.

Upon the individual's demise, his family and attorney can expedite cancellation of credit cards. This obviates the chance of improper credit charges. With knowledge of insurance policy numbers prompt inquiry can be made to the insurance companies to confirm the status of policies and beneficiaries. This also hastens the obtaining of funds. The protection of an investment position is possible by knowledge of what brokerage house and accounts are or were used, even when the regular salesmen is not known.

During ill health, another person knowing the health insurance policies concerned can help all involved. This knowledge will expedite admission procedures in the hospitals, facilitate reimbursement to a payment family member, or avoid the necessity of payment by providing for direct insurance company payment to the hospital and medical personnel.

Safe Deposit Items

"Safe deposit" usually refers to a safe deposit box in a bank. A reasonably equivalent place of safety from fire and theft could be adequate. What is reasonably equivalent will be a matter of conjecture. A heavy immovable safe in a guarded office, or a built-in wall safe in a home, can be substitutes in some instances. One fact that will enter into determining what depository is used will be the need of frequency of access. Access to a safe deposit box is governed usually by banking days and hours. This can be inconvenient.

In a safe deposit box (or other place of safety) should be placed items that are either *irreplaceable* or *inconvenient to duplicate.*

An example of the "irreplaceable" category would be bearer bonds with coupons attached for use to collect interest, family papers of sentimental value, originals of documents that have more than a record value (such as a church certificate of marriage), and even family heirlooms and jewelry that may or may not be shown or used on suitable occasions.

"Inconvenient to duplicate" items would be headed by stock certificates. A lost stock certificate can be replaced, but at a time and dollar cost and requiring the posting of a bond at a cost to obtain. Also there is the bother of form completions, and usually reminder calls to the broker or transfer agent to expedite matters. (If an estate must replace a stock certificate the matter is made more difficult by the necessity of filing current evidence of authority to act in the estate's name. When the transfer agent has been tardy in doing the paper work required of it, all that can be done is to obtain new evidence of authority at a cost and time factor.)

In addition to stock certificates there might be copies of a deed to real property such as a house and lot. This, even though the deed has been recorded at, or in, the proper office for such things.

Also, inconvenient to duplicate items would be United States savings bonds, registered bonds, and certificates of ownership to certain personal property items. ("Personal property" is loosely that which a person can take, or have taken away from the land. Even though a house can be moved, it is so awkward to move, it is considered realty.)

Other items might include animal (pet) pedigrees as well as lineage charts and other family historical summaries, for those who are interested in such data. The same lineage and pedigree history would be kept for livestock and pet animals.

Actually, to completely list items which are inconvenient to duplicate would be impossible. Much must depend upon the individual's life and needs, and what he would consider "inconvenience." Of course, with available space for safe keeping, the number and quality of items kept can be expanded.

List of Insurance Policies

To collect the benefits of an insurance policy, it is not necessary to have the policy itself. The customary keeping of a policy in the insured's safe deposit box is a misunderstood need. This is not to imply a policy should be carelessly handled. This is to note its physical presence is not essential. If a life insurance policy, by way of example, is not in hand, a "lost policy form" is completed, and along with such other documents as required for payment, such as a death certificate, this is sent to the insurance company. Payment then follows.

A list of insurance policies, with pertinent information set down, can be invaluable. If an individual has a regular insurance broker, the broker may prepare this for the individual, and then will keep a copy of the list. The information as to general (non-life insurance) policies would include what the policy covers in general terms, the amounts, the renewal dates, the premium, and the company. If a person other than the insured owns the policy, which is a term of legal significance, this would be noted.

In health insurance the same information as for general policies would be set down. Also noted would be an address and telephone number to be used for quick information and confirmation of benefits. Usually it would be a hospital or medical person who would use this.

In life insurance policies the same information as for a general policy would be noted. In addition, the fact of ownership here is vital; it can affect estate tax computation. Also added would be the names and addresses if available of the beneficiaries, both primary and contingent. ("Primary beneficiary" means that person or persons, who receives the life insurance policy benefits upon death of the insured, and "contingent beneficiary" refers to that person or persons who would receive the benefits if the primary beneficiary died before the insured.) Other notations would include whether or not the right to change beneficiaries is reserved, the form of payment selected if it has been chosen, and if this form of payment can be changed by the beneficiary.

In all instances, the place of safe-keeping of policies should be noted. Although it is not essential to have the policies (of any sort) to obtain benefits, it can be helpful to have the policy. Not only does this shorten the time and paper work, but in matters of dispute, the policy can be referred to directly.

With all the information noted, any inconsistencies as to benefits received can be considered and possibly corrected.

Service-Personnel Contacts

Every person has some individuals with whom or companies with which he deals regularly. Some of these individuals will be professional persons, such as attorneys, medical doctors, accountants, financial people, and religious leaders. The companies are likely to be insurance companies, brokerage houses, and banks (all to the extent an individual is not named). There may be other establishments related to the individual's life, personal and business.

A list of these people and companies, their addresses and telephone numbers, along with the service or function they render to the individual can be helpful. In times of need this list can be resorted to by the individual, or by another acting for him, and contact quickly made. In some instances, some of these persons will appear in the individual's personal telephone and address book under name or function. Many of the others would be known to the individual, but not listed either because use is irregular, or because the individual has no need to list a name, address and telephone number he knows by rote. But, another may not know all this.

Will and Letter of Instruction

Generally, only one copy of a will is signed by the Testator (or Testatrix) and the witnesses. This "original will," as it is termed, is kept in a safe place. The safe deposit box of the individual is considered usually such a safe place. Although some states provide for the opening of a safe deposit box for the sole purpose of making a "will search" (as it sounds, to look for a will), the application for this takes time. Therefore, a safe place might be the spouse's safe deposit box. (A spouse is the other married partner; the wife of a man, and husband of a woman). Another place would be the attorney's safe or safe deposit box, or even in some instances the office safe. In these instances, upon need, availability can be had not only by the individual, but by those surviving him.

However, copies of the will should be available in a limited number. The attorney who drew the will usually has a copy. A close family member or friend should either have a copy or have access to a copy. Any additional copies seem superfluous. A bank, if named executor or trustee, usually requests a copy. If no change in this fiduciary position is likely to be made, it is logical and proper to give it a copy.

A Letter of Instruction is another matter. More and more when a will is prepared, a Letter of Instruction is drawn. A Letter of Instruction has no legal validity. It need not be drawn by an attorney, although many do draw this as an aid to serving the client. The Letter is an immense aid in establishing and carrying out the writer's last wishes. In a Letter will appear statements such as the individual's wishes, if any, as to funeral or memorial service, what is to be done with the individual's body, where the "original will" can be found, where valuable papers are usually kept, who are this person's attorney, accountant, stock or commodity broker, religious leader, what banks are used and for what purposes, the name of the insurance broker if one is used regularly, organizations and memberships, and names of individuals who should be notified upon death.

In addition, a summary of insurance provisions, the numerical identification noted above, and other information deemed helpful in speeding along the individual's wishes appear in such a Letter. Although the individual signs this paper, this is to show it is his Letter of Instruction. The Letter, even if signed, carries no legal weight. Copies of the Letter, perhaps in an envelop marked "Open On Death" can be left not only with the individual's close family member or friend, his attorney and his religious leader, but also with other people or in other places where a copy is likely to be found. Depending on the individual and his life habits, such a place might be his office desk, his home bureau, or another place.

The thought behind preparing a Letter is that a reader can act as the writer wished. If nothing else is done but to notify those who the writer requests be notified upon death, a large step forward in carrying out the individual's wishes has been made.

Chapter VII

PREPAID LEGAL SERVICES

Prepaid legal services are plans whereby a group arranges to pay for legal services performed in behalf of its individual members. These plans are similar to group medical plans: In the same sense that group medical plans are intended to protect the employee by providing medical services when needed, prepaid legal services are intended to protect the employee by providing legal services when needed.

The Origins of Prepaid Legal Services

The federal government has long realized that there is a need for legal services for the benefit of the indigent. In the past decade, government funding was available through the Office of Economic Opportunity. This funding was in the form of grants to local nonprofit organizations, which in turn made payments to lawyers who served the eligible poor through legal aid programs. These lawyers were staff attorneys hired by the Office of Economic Opportunity.

There are other federal programs which use the services of private practitioners rather than staff attorneys to serve the indigent client. This method of delivering legal services to the poor is commonly called Judicare. The Judicare method has not been used extensively because it appears to be considerably more expensive to use private lawyers than staff attorneys.

The American Bar Association was the catalyst for the present prepaid legal services movement. The Association in 1967 appointed a committee to investigate the success of the federal programs and to determine whether a program could be developed to deliver legal services to middle income Americans.

This committee was interested in knowing who availed themselves of legal services. It found that wealthy people encountered no difficulty in finding attorneys, and the indigent could qualify for Legal Aid or similar programs. The vast majority of the population, however, did not use the services of attorneys.

101

This revelation led the American Bar Association to begin seriously investigating the possibilities of prepaid legal service programs. And in 1968 a special committee of the ABA recommended experimenting with pilot prepaid programs. Two programs were developed— one to be supervised by the Los Angeles Bar Association and the other by the Shreveport, Louisiana Bar Association. The ABA, the Ford Foundation, and employee contributions funded these pilot programs, with ABA providing the public relations support. The Shreveport program was initiated in 1971. The appendix of this volume lists the numerous plans which are now operating.

The ABA has not always been a supporter of prepaid legal services, however. Until the late 1960's, the Association through its Canon of Ethics discouraged the group prepaid legal services idea, contending that it was unethical for attorneys to participate because such a system would encourage solicitation. Most state and local bar associations also opposed it, and some still do.

Until very recently, the Code of Professional Responsibility of the American Bar Association did not cover prepaid legal services. But in early 1974 the Code was revised to treat the ethical considerations of an attorney accepting work through a prepaid legal service program.

Advantages of Prepaid Legal Services

Prepaid legal plans provide legal services for a great number of people at a small cost per person. These programs operate on the time-honored insurance concept of sharing the cost among a great many to protect the few who may require assistance.

Prepaid plans will encourage "preventive law"—that is, people will be more likely to consult attorneys before a crisis arises. When the pitfalls and potential hazards of an agreement are pointed out in advance, problems can be avoided.

Open and Closed Panel Programs

An open-panel program permits the employee to choose any lawyer in the community who is willing to be a participant under the prepaid legal service program. Generally, this would include the majority of practicing attorneys.

A closed panel is organized by the administrators of the program or the employee's union. In a closed-panel system, there is no freedom of choice. The employee must avail himself of a lawyer or group of lawyers that is submitted to him. This is like many medical group programs.

Funding of Prepaid Plans

Usually the employer and employee contribute jointly to a prepaid legal service plan, but sometimes only the employee contributes.

Type of Legal Services Covered

Coverage for members varies with the input of dollars. At the low end of the scale, the Amalgamated Clothing Workers of Chicago has instituted a plan that costs its members 50 cents per month. The range of benefits is limited to minor legal problems. The cost can go as high as $10 per month when coverage is broad.

Plans usually cover investigation, including obtaining witness statements, determining whether an action should be brought, and discussing the facts of the case with other parties involved. Most plans do not cover income tax returns.

The plan may specify a maximum charge for each service rendered (e.g., $250 for a legal separation or $50 for a will). There is always a maximum total dollar limit for the year. The limit ranges from about $1,000 to $3,000.

In addition to dollar limits, some plans will also limit the number of consultations for which an individual member can collect. Coverage will be limited to a specified number of office hours or a specified number of consultations.

APPENDIX
Table 1

1. Groups Covered by Self-contained Legal Service Plans

(Not included: group consultation and referral plans; groups served by third-party risk carrier; student plans; automobile clubs)

Name and Address of Plan or Group	Nature of Group	Risk Carrier	Administrator	Remarks (Special Characteristics)
1. AFSCME Local 101 Legal Services Plan San Jose CA	union members (city employees)	law firm	law firm	agreement with law firm; advice and consultation only
2. Akron Teachers Credit Union, Inc. 645 N. Main St. Akron OH 44310	credit union members	law firm	group	agreement with law firm; voluntary participation; unlimited consultation; wills
3. Alaska Teamsters	union members	trust fund	trustees	joint trust fund
4. Chicago Joint Board, Amalgamated Clothing Workers 333 S. Ashland Blvd. Chicago IL 60607	union members	law firm	law firm	agreement with law firm; voluntary participation
5. California Teachers Association 1705 Murchison Dr. Burlingame CA 94010	teachers	association	association	employment related matters covered by association, others referred to participating attorneys
6. CEA Legal Services Fund (Bay City MI)	union members (city employees)	trust fund	Group 50 306 Townsend St. Lansing MI 48933	union plan; designed with cooperation of state bar; free choice of attorney
7. Central Louisiana Plumbers & Steamfitters Legal Service Plan 4012 Parliament Dr. Alexandria LA 71301	union members	trust fund	trustees	joint trust fund; free choice of attorney

105

	Name and Address of Plan or Group	Nature of Group	Risk Carrier	Administrator	Remarks (Special Characteristics)
8.	City of Columbus Employees (AFSCME Local 1632) (Columbus OH)	union members (city employees)	Ohio Legal Services Fund 33 W. 11th Ave. Columbus OH 43201	carrier	contract between city and trust fund; free choice of attorney
9.	Columbus Education Association 700 E. Broad St. Columbus OH 43215	teachers	law firm	law firm	agreement with law firm; extended consultation and referral
10.	Consumers' Group Legal Services, Inc. 1414 University Ave. Berkeley CA 94702	co-op members	group	group	extended consultation and referral
11.	Cooperative Group Legal Service 2023 W. Stadium Blvd. Ann Arbor MI 48103	co-op members	law firm	group	agreement with law firm; consultation and referral
12.	District Council 33, AFSCME Philadelphia PA	union members (city employees)	trust fund	trustees	union plan; staff attorneys
13.	District Council 37, AFSCME 140 Park Place New York NY 10007	union members (city employees)	Municipal Employees Legal Services Fund	fund	union plan; staff attorneys and social workers
14.	District Council 47, AFSCME Philadelphia PA	union members (city employees)	law firm	law firm	agreement with law firm
15.	Green Bay Education Association 1142 Main St. Green Bay WI 54301	teachers	association	association	agreement with law firm; extended consultation and referral
16.	Int'l Org. of Masters, Mates & Pilots 39 Broadway New York NY 10006	union members	trust fund	trustees	joint labor-management trust fund; attorneys selected by trustees for representation in Coast Guard hearings

106

Name and Address of Plan or Group	Nature of Group	Risk Carrier	Administrator	Remarks Special) (Characteristics)
17. Laborers' Legal Services Laborers' District Council of Washington, D.C. & Vicinity 805 15th St., NW Washington DC 20005	union members	plan	plan	union plan; staff attorneys
18. Laborers' Local 229 Legal Service Plan P.O. Box 4523 2620 Centenary Shreveport LA 71104	union members	trust fund	Southwest Administrators	union plan with trust fund; free choice of attorney
19. Laborers' Local 423 Legal Service Plan 620 Alum Creek Dr. Columbus OII 43205	union members	union	union	union plan; staff attorney
20. Laborers' Local 559 Legal Service Plan P.O. Box 1211 Birmingham AL 35201	union members	law firm	union	union plan; staff attorney
21. Maine Teachers Legal Services Plan 35 Community Dr. Augusta ME C4330	teachers	association	association	voluntary plan; staff attorneys
22. Massachusetts Laborers' Legal Services Fund One Gateway Center Newton MA 02158	union members	trust fund	fund	union plan; staff attorney

Name and Address of Plan or Group	Nature of Group	Risk Carrier	Administrator	Remarks (Special Characteristics)
23. Michigan Education Association	teachers	Michigan Education Association Legal Services Corp. 306 Townsend St. Lansing MI 48933	Group 50	carrier jointly controlled by teachers association and bar association
24. Millwrights and Machinery Erectors Local 1454 1228 Walnut St. Cincinnati OH 45210	union members	law firm	union and law firm	agreement with law firm
25. Minnesota Education Association Legal Services Benefit Plan 41 Sherburne Ave. St. Paul MN 55103	teachers	association	association and Minnesota Indemnity, Inc.	cooperation with Minnesota State Bar Association and with Minnesota Indemnity, Inc.; free choice of attorney
26. Rhode Island Public Service Employees' Legal Service Plan (Laborers' Local 1033) 40 Westminster St. Suite 1720 Providence RI 02903	union members (city employees)	trust fund	trustees	union plan; attorneys selected by trustees
27. Teamsters Local 20 Legal Defense Fund 435 S. Hawley St. Toledo OH 43609	union members	union	union	union plan; extended consultation and referral; attorneys selected by union
28. Truck Drivers Local 807 New York NY	union members	trust fund	trustees	joint labor-management trust fund; attorneys selected by trustees
29. Yonkers Teamsters Welfare Fund Prepaid Services Plan 160 S. Central Ave. Elsford NY 10533	union members	trust fund	law firm	joint labor-management trust fund; agreement with single attorney

108

2. Carriers Offering Legal Service Coverages

	Name and Address	Legal Form	Sponsored by	Groups Covered	Remarks
1.	Arizona Legal Services, Inc. P.O. Box 7283 Phoenix AZ 85011	nonprofit corporation	bar association	employee groups, automobile club	cooperation agreement with Midwest Mutual
2.	California Lawyers' Service P.O. Box 26231 San Francisco CA 94126	nonprofit corporation	bar association	none	
3.	Colorado Legal Care Society 1117 Cherokee St. Denver CO 80204	nonprofit corporation	bar association	state employees	cooperation agreement with Midwest Mutual
4.	Consumers' Group Legal Services, Inc. 1414 University Ave. Berkeley CA 94702	nonprofit corporation	co-op	co-op members	contemplates expansion
5.	Cumis Insurance Society, Inc. 5910 Mineral Point Rd. Madison WI 53705	insurance company		credit union in Colorado	
6.	Employers Mutual Liability Ins. Co. of Wisconsin 2000 Westwood Dr. Wausau WI 54401	insurance company		none	
7.	Equal Justice, Inc. (Chicago Bar Association) 179 W. Washington St. Chicago IL 60602	nonprofit corporation	bar association	none	
8.	Insurance Company of North America 1600 Arch St. Philadelphia PA 19101	insurance company		none	

	Name and Address	Legal Form	Sponsored by	Groups Covered	Remarks
9.	Michigan Education Association Legal Services Corp. 306 Townsend St. Lansing MI 48933	nonprofit corporation	teachers association and bar association	members of teachers association	
10.	Midwest Mutual Ins. Co. Legal Protection Ins. Div. 13315 San Antonio Dr. Norwalk CA 90650	insurance company		groups in several states	cooperation agreements with several bar-sponsored nonprofit organizations
11.	National Independence Ins. Co. Liberty Park Frazer PA 19355	insurance company		none	
12.	New York County Lawyers' Ass'n Prepaid Legal Services Plan 25 Broad St. New York NY 10004	nonprofit corporation	bar association	none	
13.	North Carolina Prepaid Legal Services Corp. P.O. Box 25246 Raleigh NC 27611	nonprofit corporation	bar association	employee groups	
14.	Ohio Legal Services Fund 33 W. 11th Ave. Columbus OH 43201	trust fund	bar association	city of Columbus employees	
15.	Oregon Prepaid Legal Ins., Inc. 1109 Cascade Bldg. 520 S.W. 6th Ave. Portland OR 97202	nonprofit corporation	bar association	employee group	cooperation agreement with Midwest Mutual

110

	Name and Address	Legal Form	Sponsored by	Groups Covered	Remarks
16.	Prepaid Legal Services of Idaho 225 N. 16th St. P.O. Box 5597 Boise ID 83705	unincorporated division of state bar	bar association	credit union	
17.	Prepaid Legal Services of Kansas, Inc. P.O. Box 1856 Wichita KS 67201	nonprofit corporation	bar association	employee groups, student groups, credit union, fraternal credit card company	
18.	Prepaid Legal Services Corp. of New Mexico 1117 Stanford, N.E. Albuquerque NM 87131	nonprofit corporation	bar association	1 credit union, 1 teachers association, state employees	cooperation agreement with Midwest Mutual
19.	Prepaid Legal Services, Inc., of St. Louis 705 Olive St. St. Louis MO 63101	nonprofit corporation	bar association	none	
20.	Professional Motor Service Club, Inc. P.O. Box 145 Ada OK 74820	motor service club		employee groups, teachers, Indian tribes	operating like an insurance company although organized as a motor club
21.	Ranger Ins. Co. P.O. Box 2807 Houston TX 77001	insurance company		none	
22.	St. Paul Fire & Marine Ins. Co. 385 Washington St. St. Paul MN 55102	insurance company		none	

111

	Name and Address	Legal Form	Sponsored by	Groups Covered	Remarks
23.	Stonewall Ins. Co. 2308 4th Ave. Birmingham AL 35203	insurance company		1 credit union, 2 employee groups	
24.	Stuyvesant Ins. Co. 1105 Hamilton St. Allentown PA 18101	insurance company		none	
25.	Suffolk County Legal Services Corporation 4175 Veterans Memorial Hwy. Ronkonkoma NY 11779	nonprofit corporation	bar association	none	
26.	Texas Legal Protection Plan, Inc. James R. Dougherty Memorial Bldg. Colorado at Fifteenth Austin TX 78711	nonprofit corporation	bar association	employee and teachers groups	
27.	Utah Prepaid Legal Services Plan 1706 Major St. Salt Lake City UT 84115	nonprofit corporation	bar association	credit union	
28.	Washington Lawyers Service c/o Northwest Administrators, Inc. 2300 Eastlake Ave. E Seattle WA 98102	nonprofit corporation	bar association	employee group	

INDEX

113

114

115